The Things We Know

But Do Not Do

Thank You
for believing in
me and what I do!
Remember, "It's All About
the Why"

The Things We Know

But Do Not Do

Insights into Parenting, Teaching and Coaching Today's Youth

Jayson Wells

ISBN: 978-1-944662-37-0

Publishing date: July 2019

Cover Design by Michael Scott, MASgraphicarts.com

5

Dedication

This book is dedicated to Mr. Donald Edward Wells, the man responsible for bringing me into this world, and the two grandsons he never got a chance to meet. His teachings are what led to the insights of this book, and the backbone of who I am as a man, father and coach. My father instilled the quality traits that would not only allow me to pursue significance and purpose, but also allow me to share those principles with others. Every piece of wisdom in this book was introduced to me at home first. I believe that's how it should be. Wisdom starts at home and is watered, nurtured and cultivated throughout life. Daddy, I love you, I miss you, and I thank you for planting the seeds for me to grow into a strong rooted tree that will also bear fruit to nourish the world.

Jaylen and Jaydon, you are the direct fruit from the tree your Grandpa Donald planted. I know that circumstances out of your control restrict our physical time together but know that you get every bit of wisdom that I received. I wrote this book so you could know a little piece of your Grandpa by knowing more about me. I am who I am because he was such a great man. I am committed to taking what he taught me and expanding on them with things I've learned in my life, to make sure you are armed with what you will need to navigate through this wonderfully crazy life! I want you both to know that whatever you decide to pursue on a personal, educational, or occupational level will be supported by me. If it's athletics, I will teach you everything I know. If it's something outside of my knowledge, I will encourage, support and cheer you on, just as my dad did with me. I love you guys more than anything. Always remember to D.E.W. YOU!!

Foreword

Connection (noun): "A relationship in which a person, thing, or idea is linked or associated with something else." That's the definition according to Webster's Dictionary (2019). Jayson Wells and I met in 2012 while working with an international brand that was more in alignment with his career as an international professional basketball star rather than my career as a certified therapist. Soon we'd find out just how much we had in common, not only as professionals but also as men.

It all happened as a classic crossroads moment; I was considering a new career path and Jayson had just retired in 2011, a year prior to our initial introduction. We indulged in the proverbial salutations and small talk as in the who, what, why, when, and where, and as it turns out, it was the where that would start us on the road to becoming fast friends. Jayson was a kid from Cleveland, Ohio, 93rd and Union to be exact, and I was just a kid from Akron, a stone's throw down the road. After running through the W's (what I like to call them), it was the Y that would solidify our friendship and start Jayson down the path as an author, speaker, and storyteller.

I remember Jayson calling me in tears after just having had a conversation with his wonderful mother and sharing what seemed to be an epiphany as to the reason she incorporated a Y in his name. See, what I've come to realize is that everything happens for a reason, and everything and everyone is connected in some form or fashion. In *The Things We Know But Do Not Do*, Jayson confirms that ideological concept with easy-to-digest examples and experiences that make it impossible to not at least give long and thoughtful consideration as to why or why not something is true.

I had the privilege of overhearing a conversation where Jayson was sharing with someone that the distance between your head and your heart is a mere eighteen inches. He went on to simplify his reasoning for writing *The Things We Know But Do Not Do* as an example of just that, a matter of inches. This book lends itself to the juxtaposition of where you are and where you want to be; closing the gap, the distance, and the disconnect, making your dreams just that much more attainable.

Indulge in *The Things We Know But Do Not Do* to find your Y. Make the connections by closing the gaps in your personal, professional, and spiritual relationships and taking the steps required to stay the course.

Paul Ware Jr.
Catalyst of Inspiration

Contents

Introduction

I'm so glad you picked up this book! Although I've never met you, I know we will become fast friends as you read through its pages. My goal is to Inspire, Impact and Ignite you through my stories, examples, and information so my hope is that you will have many ah-ha moments as you ingest and digest the rich, succulent food I'm about to serve you.

My travels across the globe playing basketball and now speaking have been wrought with both struggles and triumphs but along the way I've been able to inspire youth and adults through my personal mission to:

Develop. Extraordinary. Winners.

Reading this book will give you access to the same information I share with audiences so you, too, can become an extraordinary winner in life.

Early in my basketball career, warming the bench way more often than I would have liked proved to be the training ground to test my commitment. Did I *really* want to play that bad? Would I *ever* be better than the more experienced players? I knew I had it in me but I was in the crucible of waiting, yet those years of waiting and wanting and preparing tested my commitment to the core and also ignited a raging fire inside that could not be quenched. I learned about potential. I learned about tenacity. I learned what it takes to become the best version of me both as a person and as a player. I learned how to harness that raging personal fire, refine it, and then release it out into the world in the form of speaking and conducting workshops to individuals, teams and organizations.

What you're going to learn throughout these pages will help ignite your internal fire, allow you to discover your true purpose, and show you how you can create your own legacy from a place of knowing how significant you really are.

Are you ready? Let's go!

The L.A.B.

Leadership through Athletics & Business

Ball is Life

Over the past few years I've heard constantly that athletes and ex-military are highly sought after in the work world. I now know why! The PRINCIPLES you learn and apply every day in those two environments are priceless!

I've been playing basketball on an organized basketball team since seventh grade. Those first two years of organized ball almost broke me. There would have been no high school ball, no college ball and definitely no professional ball if it were up to me. I wanted to quit the team! Not because I wasn't good, but because I DID NOT like playing for my father! He was my coach back then and playing for him was one of the toughest things in the world. Come to find out, it was a two-way street, because as tough as it was for me to play for my dad, it was equally as tough for him to coach me.

See, when you're coaching your child, for the most part there is no cheering or being a regular dad and your child's biggest fan, because there is always someone who will criticize and say loud enough for anyone to hear that coach is playing favorites. And, conversely, it's awfully difficult for a twelve-year-old to forget the fact that he just got chewed out by coach, but now "coach" is sitting at the dinner table!

All that is to say that the foundation of a VALUE system and PRINCIPLES taught at home, and taught in athletics, is a tremendous tool for a young person's toolbox. Attitude, work ethic, discipline, how to work as a team, how to lead, how to be led, trust, integrity, commitment...man, I get goosebumps just writing those things! Isn't that what life is about? Great coaches and teachers constantly reinforcing those and other great values in young athletes and students. Learning and applying a value system is not something that is just Mom and Dad's job, nor is it simply a coach's or teacher's job.

It is the job of whoever is influential in a young person's life!

"It takes a village," as my Big Mama (Grandma) used to say. But somewhere that has gotten lost. I witness parents getting upset when coach "oversteps his boundaries" and includes LIFE lessons into the sport. Or worse yet, coach doesn't care as long as he gets his conference championship. We wonder why society is the way it is. Maybe it's because there is very little accountability across the board as adults because we are bickering at each other and ultimately neglecting the kids!

I once watched a documentary on Earvin "Magic" Johnson. He told a story about his dad who was a sanitation worker. Young Earvin was helping his dad and in the rush of being cold, and eager to finish, did a half-hearted job picking up a garbage can. "Before I could even get back into the truck, Dad had pulled me out and told me to pick up all the scraps I missed! He said that if I could not commit to doing a job whole-heartedly, I didn't need that job." Johnson decided to apply that lesson to his basketball career, and we all know where that took him!

Attention young people! If you have the privilege of being an athlete, no matter your skill level or place on the team, dedicate yourself to the constant pursuit of improvement; every game, every practice, every play. You may never excel at that particular sport, but I can guarantee when you face obstacles in "real life," you will have the familiarity of going through battles already, and the comfort of knowing what it takes to overcome them!

The values I've learned on the basketball court have made me the man I am today.

Don't lose yourself before you even find yourself! It is truly more than a game if you approach it that way! Coaches, teachers, parents: Instill in these young people hardcore values that will go with them to the NBA, the Executive Boardroom, or whatever career path they may choose. Because at the end of the day it doesn't matter what you do if you haven't invested in the personal development to support it!

Big Ballin'

Who Ball? We Ball!! LaVar Ball, Lonzo Ball, Melo and Gelo Ball. You can't be involved in the basketball world and not hear their names in some capacity. *LaVar is crazy. Lonzo is a bust. Gelo is a thief. Melo is just a young kid trapped by fame and a boisterous dad.* These are some of the things being said about the family. Whatever your opinion is, there is one thing for certain: The Balls are all household names!

As I listen to ESPN, NBA TV and other sports news programs I can't help but get nervous about the fact that as of this writing LaVar is sending his eighteen-year-old and fifteen-year-old sons overseas to play as professionals. It's understandable that some fans are confused because of their age, experience and quite frankly how LaVar has gone about handling the situation. To me, the situation is extremely intriguing for a couple different reasons. 1) I was barely twenty-one years old in 1998 when I first went overseas. 2) I have a genuine interest in the success of the game of basketball and the image we provide to our next generation of players and business people.

The biggest difference between 1998 and now is simple. In 1998, playing overseas was still "taboo" to most American players, especially the SUPERSTARS. No way was Michael Jordan, Shaquille O'Neal, or a young Kobe Bryant going overseas to play anything outside the Olympics. Now, with the influx of quality foreign players and the exposure to international basketball, everyone and their uncle will *entertain* offers. What many of these guys don't understand is that international basketball IS NOT THE NBA! You WILL NOT drive a fancy car, you WILL NOT stay at five-star hotels, and most importantly YOU WILL practice every day, no excuses, or you'll find yourself on a plane headed back home, wondering what happened! I think guys go into this thinking, "Oh I went overseas with my college for two weeks; I know what international ball is about." WRONG! That is a vacation compared to LIVING somewhere for eight to nine months of the year. And sometimes it doesn't hit you until you realize, "Man…I can't go to Waffle House, In'-N-Out Burger, or get my favorite cereal from the store!"

Make sure you keep an eye on the continuing Ball boys saga because often it's not playing ball that's the issue, it's life outside of the court that becomes difficult to handle! The Ball boys' overseas experience didn't last very long—three months to be exact. In fact, the ending involved LaVar Ball pulling the boys off the team and out of the league with two regular season games left. So now, the boys have surrendered their college eligibility because they've been paid as professionals, Gelo has realized that he's just not good enough, and Melo is going to continue his professional career in Australia for the upcoming season. This is quickly becoming a horror story, when it could have been one of the best times of their lives, doing what they love and seeing parts of the world they never even knew existed! That's experience talking! I'm just a little boy from Cleveland who has traveled to six continents!

Did It!

Phil Knight is the co-founder and chairman of Nike. As a child, Knight discovered he had a love for running and went to the University of Oregon to enhance his skills with legendary track coach Bill Bowerman. In addition to coaching, Bowerman was experimenting with creating new types of shoes and Knight tested them on the track.

After graduating, Knight went to graduate school at Stanford and signed up for a small business class where he had to create a business plan. He remembered Bowerman's shoes. In his business plan, Knight created the blueprint for superior athletic shoes which could be produced cheaply in Japan. After taking a job as an accountant to make his father happy, and hating it, Knight flew to Japan to find a company to make his shoes. He returned home and created a partnership with Bowerman, each of them investing $500. Their original business name was Blue Ribbon Sports but later they changed it to Nike. In its first year, the company sold only $364 worth of shoes, but Knight was determined to make the company work and stuck with it until it did.

Today, Nike brings in almost $30 billion in revenue and Knight's stake in the company gives him an estimated net worth of $13 billion dollars. By having the courage to leave the job his father wanted him to have, Knight was able to start his own business and eventually build one of the most recognizable companies in the world. I recently read Phil's book, Shoe Dog, and I've come up with three action items that we all can learn from Knight on how to pursue our dreams and make our visions become reality.

1. **Have a clear focus:** Many times, it's hard to stick to your path when you're not getting the momentum you were hoping for or when things seem to be falling apart around you. But almost everybody must go through those dark days in order to get to the light at the end of the tunnel. You must have the faith and courage to stick to your vision and stay completely focused on the goal of what you set out to do. As Nike grew Knight had to decide what the focus of his business would be. Should he get into the fashion business? Should he expand and sponsor other celebrities since he had such success sponsoring athletes? Knight decided that for his company to continue growing, he would have to have a clear focus on what he wanted the company to be. It would make it easier for him to make decisions and allow his team to work toward a common goal. According to Knight, "We wanted Nike to be the best sports and fitness company in the world."

   Like Nike, once you have your why, you have your direction and North Star!

2. **Think of business as war:** The business world is very competitive, and some industries are more cutthroat than others. If you're offering a new product or service that you're hoping will take customers away from your competition, you can expect those competitors to fight back. Develop a plan to beat them and start winning their market share. As a former athlete, Knight came to love competition and relish the chance to compete in the business world. He treats business as war and instilled within his company a healthy dislike of its competitors by always trying to one up them. When Reebok went to the expense of sponsoring the entire Olympic Games, Nike sponsored just the top athletes but gained much more valuable coverage than its competition.

It was also Knight's competitive streak that made him want to sign a twenty-year-old Stanford golfer named Tiger Woods before his competition could. It cost Knight over forty million dollars, but it was well worth the price tag to keep his golfing prodigy out of the hands of his competitors. Nike is a very competitive organization and Knight wouldn't have it any other way. According to Knight, "Sports is natural, instinctive, competitive and in the end, rewarding. All of us at Nike get to earn a living in that world. A world that is easy to believe in. Business is war without bullets."

3. **Did it!:** The single thing that differentiates go-getters from everyone else is that go-getters go for it. "We left the security of a steady paycheck to venture into the unknown for our chance to determine our own destiny" says Knight. We need to keep that attitude in mind as we grow our dreams and visions. Don't be afraid of making mistakes. You won't be able to do anything significant if there isn't a risk of failure. Nike is known for its slogan Just Do It and it's a statement that accurately reflects how Phil Knight acts as a businessman. He's always taking chances, willing to fail and push the conventional limits to accomplish his goals. A great example of this is his relationship with Michael Jordan. In 1984, Knight and Nike signed Jordan to a sponsorship deal. The big risk was that Jordan was only twenty-one years old and just breaking into the league. The idea of individual players being sponsored was also a new phenomenon and was a risky and unproven concept. The deal proved to be a huge success for Nike and provided publicity and a sales boost for the company. If Knight had been afraid to Just Do It, or if he had been afraid to make a mistake, the deal would've never happened.

According to Knight, "The trouble nowadays is that we're making too few mistakes rather than going out, taking risks and learning from the mistakes we make."

I have been blessed to have had the opportunity to work with Nike for the past seven years on the Elite Basketball side. I've been able to work with top high school, college and professional players and coaches. The most awesome part about my entire experience is the fact that I've been able to learn, grow and develop indirectly from a man I haven't even had the chance to meet in person yet. But, I'm grateful for the fact that I was a Nike man before I was a "Nike man." And, by the way, trendsetters never settle as we'll see in the next chapter.

D.E.W. YOU

The Settlers

Remember those commercials? The family of "settlers" who won't get Direct TV because they settle for cable. They were funny and most definitely caught our attention. There's a reason that those commercials resonate with us so much.

Let's face it, we all settle in some area of our lives. However, I want to tackle two major areas that can put us on the course for a long, treacherous life ahead. These two areas are in our relationships and in our occupations.

Relationships

I will preface with this: I'm not talking about when we were twenty-one-year-olds and we thought the person we were with was going to be with us forever even though NOTHING really lined up with our feelings. Nor am I referring to your partner liking alternative rock music and you liking R&B. I'm speaking of those things in a relationship that should be deal breakers. For example, VALUES! If you don't share the same values as your partner, it's only a matter of time before it gets to a point where it's unbearable. These could be parental values, financial values, or even relationship values. Two people having different outlooks on something as crucial as what they believe are in for a long road of frustration.

Another area we should be extremely careful of in our relationships are our pursuit of goals and visions. Not having common ground in your values can turn out to be disastrous! A person who has big goals and truly has a desire to meet them will usually be focused, disciplined and determined to reach those goals. Meanwhile, if their partner doesn't share a similar level of intensity and drive, at some point, one or both is going to get frustrated; upset because the drive isn't there, or because they don't understand why there's so much determination and so little time.

Occupations

This one is very sensitive to me because I understand that to many people, I've lived (and probably still do live) a "dream life" when it comes to my job. That perception comes from someone on the outside looking in. They don't understand the demands on an athlete's body, mind and spirit. They just see "the life" and think every waking second reflects a charmed life. Now don't get me wrong, I understand that I am part of a very small percentage of people who get to say, "Basketball is my job." Because our jobs are based on a series of relationships, our occupation falls under one big relationship and VALUES play a huge part in a long-lasting work partnership. I recently had to part ways in some business relationships because our values didn't line up. It's difficult to "break up," as it is in a personal relationship, but what you want to ask yourself when that happens is, "Would I rather deal with the difficulty upfront or deal with being unhappy forever?" Mmmm, something to ponder...and act on if necessary.

So, why do we settle for relationships that don't fulfill us and occupations that don't feed our soul? Simply put, I believe it's because IT'S EASY and COMFORTABLE! We settle in our personal relationships because we think, *I've been with this person for so long already*, or *I'm older now and want to be in a relationship so I'm just going to align myself with someone who fills that void*," and let's not leave out, *because the physical attraction is so high*. We've all been there!

Likewise, we settle in our occupations because *the money is good,* or *it's the job I've had all my life and I don't want to take the time to learn another field,* and perhaps the worst one, *I'm working this job because everyone else wants me to, so I have to maintain expectations.*

GARBAGE!

Do what makes *you* happy, do what makes *you* fulfilled, be with someone who motivates, encourages, pushes, AND supports *you*! Who came up with the philosophy that we must settle in order to have a "normal" life? We often hear from those around us that we must either make the money and hate our job OR love what we do and get paid pennies. Well, maybe the hardcore truth lies right there—I don't want a "normal" life! I want an EXTRAORDINARY life, and for that to happen, I refuse to do ordinary things, like settle in my life for a toxic person OR an occupation that drains my soul!

I heard a very interesting statistic from my business coach, Simon Sinek. He said over ninety percent of people come home from work each day unhappy and unfulfilled! That's ridiculous! I find it very difficult to understand how someone goes to work every day, for thirty years, hating their job. Imagine what kind of energy those people are bringing home to their families. I would add to that statement by saying I believe almost the same number of people are unhappy and unfulfilled in their relationships. So where does that leave us? It leaves us with a bunch of people who hate their jobs and hate their relationships, which are the two areas where we spend most of our time and energy. And where do all these unhappy people interact? On our local streets, roads and highways. So, no wonder there's so much road rage and hostility while we're out and about. A bunch of unhappy people, leaving a workplace they hate, going to a relationship place they hate.

Imagine if ninety percent of people enjoyed and felt fulfilled at their jobs. What would that look like? The ninety percent would naturally be happier when engaging with other people in the workplace, and, in turn, the people they engaged with would be happier. Out of that would emerge a corporate culture of people spreading positive energy through interaction. The same ninety percent would then go home, and because they feel happy having generated positive energy in their workplace would carry their positivity into their personal relationships. And now here we are in a seemingly impossible world where people genuinely like and enjoy each other! It's SIMPLE, but not necessarily easy. The first step is for us to stop settling in our lives! After all, maybe Direct TV isn't so bad. The opposite of settling is taking action which is our focus for the next chapter.

Time for Some Action

Those of you who know me, know that for the past five years on New Year's Day I commit to "one word" as opposed to making a list of typical New Year resolutions. I've never been a big resolutions guy and after reading Jon Gordon's book, *One Word*, I was convinced that my word for 2018 was *JUMP*. I am committed to "jumping" in my decision-making, trusting my faith and intentionally searching for situations that will force me to jump.

All the famous people you hear about—Will Smith, Steve Harvey, Gary Vaynerchuk—are no different than you are. Seventy percent of the world's millionaires are "self-made" which means YOU can achieve what you want just like they did. It's not going to be easy—you're not going to wake up on Monday and then become wealthy on Tuesday—but becoming wildly successful and wealthy doesn't take any more effort than going to a job that you hate!

It's been said, "All you have to do is think, believe in your heart, and you'll achieve." THAT'S NOT TRUE! There are a lot of people who think wonderful, great thoughts. They believe they deserve life's treasures, but they fail to do one MAJOR thing... TAKE CONSISTENT ACTION!! Most people aren't willing to commit to exchanging what's comfortable to what's uncomfortable long enough for a new habit to form!

I've been asked dozens of times, "Why aren't you the stereotypical kid from the inner city? Why aren't you in that pool?" The answer is, I made a CHOICE! I made a choice that I did not want to be the poor, directionless street kid from the inner city. There's nothing special about me. But I can tell you that extraordinary things have happened for me and to me because of making a choice to be better, do better. So, as you think to yourself about all the choices you've made and how your life is all over the place, decide now to make ONE different choice. Just one.

Anything we want to achieve starts in the mind with one decision. After we make that decision in our mind, then we get our bodies to move in tandem with our mind and we begin to create. Only YOU control YOUR life! I truly believe that our lives are controlled by one force, DECISIONS. Of course, I believe in a Supreme Being, greater than myself. But I also believe that our Supreme Being gives us the power of choice and the decisions we make control us much more than the conditions we face. It's not your conditions, it's your decisions!

It's not security that robs ambition, it's the ILLUSION of security that robs ambition, which means the biggest risk you can take in life is NOT taking one at all. Wayne Gretzky would agree as he has been quoted many times as saying, "You miss 100% of the shots you don't take."

If you're in the middle of your career and you hate your job, or you're barely out of high school or college and just starting, go find someone over sixty to talk to about what they really regret about their lives. You will discover that none of them regret what they failed at; their biggest regrets stem from the things that they didn't try. It's the "Why didn't I?" they regret most.

You cannot let the fear of others' opinions influence your decisions. Most people who are bold in verbalizing their opinions typically have not honored their dreams and that causes them to transmit their fear onto others—a fear that comes from realizing they will die knowing they didn't fulfill their dreams because of choices they made or didn't make. Remember, it's YOUR life!

Nobody else can tell you what's best for you and only you will have to deal with the consequences, so make your own decisions!

To be fulfilled, your occupation must align with what you truly love. If you don't truly love what you do in your workplace, DON'T DO IT! Sometimes you may have to work transitional jobs to get to where you want. The adage is true, "Do what you *have* to do, so you can do what you *want* to do." For example, I sold water meters to apartment complexes for a year, but I did what I *had* to and learned to do my work with pride, but at the same time I didn't allow that "good enough for now" job to kill my dream because I knew the only thing that could make me feel alive was clinging to my dream!

Don't let anyone steer you away from where you want to be in life; not your parents, not your teachers, not your coaches, friends or family. If you have a passion for a specific occupation and you feel confident that you can do it, go after it! This is YOUR life, you have the tools and resources to make it happen, and living your goal will energize you in that each morning you'll wake up knowing that you are blessed and possess an opportunity that most people in life do not have. You have the ability to live your dreams. It's on YOU to make sure you do.

When We Were Kids

I believe you were born a genius. You have awesome potential inside you! Science talks about how little of our brain's power we use over the course of our lives, but remember when you were a little kid? You had a fire in your belly! When you were a little kid, you didn't have a problem connecting with other human beings. When you were a little kid, you were an artist. When you were a little kid, you didn't care what other people thought; you were super comfortable in your own skin. When you were a little kid, you wanted to be an astronaut, a professional athlete, President of the United States, a billionaire, or someone who would change the world. When you were a little kid, you spoke your truth. When you were a little kid, you had amazing amounts of energy. Recall how you were as a kid, or other kids you've been around—kids don't walk anywhere... THEY RUN! When you were a little kid, you weren't serious, you loved to play, and that was your natural state. You didn't have to be forced or motivated...you just were. But then life comes along...

Here's what I believe happens. From the moment you are born you start picking up the messaging of mass thinking. You start receiving a kind of hypnosis from the world around you. If your mom fears money because she has money issues, she will say, "Money doesn't grow on trees" even though she's well intentioned as your mom. If your dad has been burned by people, he will say, "Be careful and don't trust people." When you go to school, what do your teachers tell you? "Dress like everyone else, think like everyone else, don't laugh too loud, don't be creative, geniuses are cut from a different cloth, don't think too big, play small." Then you start making friends and they, along with others, start laughing at your dreams. Then society and the media start giving you its mass thinking mentality that sends a message to submit to a *life of average* by spending the best years of your life watching television in a subdivision. They tell you that you can't be healthy like an athlete, you can't be optimistic like an "A" player, you can't build a great company, or a great team, or the house of your dreams, or change the world, or find the love that you want. "Resign yourself to mediocrity" is the message mass media delivers to you your entire life. Then we get surprised when we're twenty years old, or thirty-five or fifty-five or eighty-five, and we have programmed ourselves at a deep level through daily repetition from the world around us to disbelieve in ourselves, to disbelieve that we're a genius and to disbelieve in our dreams.

So many of us wake up every day in fear. We wake up scared, scared to leave the box. We work in a box, we drive to work in a box, we eat lunch out of a box, we go home and live in a box, we spend five hours every day watching a box, and then we die in a box and call it a life. My intent, my passion, my promise to you, is to remind you that you're not supposed to live your life in a box and then die in a box. I'm here to remind you to not believe the mass thinking. Eleanor Roosevelt said, "The future belongs to those who believe in the beauty of their dreams." She was correct! And then there's Malcolm X who said, "The future belongs to those who prepare for it today." To prepare yourself for your dream, you are the architect today and every day. YOU get to decide who and when and how and where! Others don't get to decide. Live YOUR dream! Be YOU, Love YOU, D.E.W. YOU!

You Better Get That Lesson

This chapter's title is a slight play on words, and here's why:

1. To my young supporters, you should listen and learn from the wisdom that older people provide.

2. A shout out to all those with grandmothers like mine who call homework or schoolwork "lessons."

I am smart...book smart, street smart, common sense smart... all that. But what does all that smartness benefit me if I don't use it, but instead allow the pursuit of all things unimportant to corrupt my intelligence? My grades all the way through my freshman year at Indiana State were always good, or at least decent; my definition of decent being about a 2.5 GPA. But during my sophomore year I started a downward spiral that I would not recover from until I was significantly past due for my degree. Why would that happen when I was so smart? Who knows? Pick the thought of the day. *I'm cool now, I'm the star of the basketball team so I can't be perceived as nerdy."* Or how about this one? *"I am the star of the team, my teachers CAN'T fail me."* And don't forget the most famous. *"I'm gonna play pro, why do I need a degree?"* At this point in my life I can't go back and listen to the people who told me to make sure I kept my grades right, or make sure I got my degree. As I look back, I now understand why I didn't listen initially—it was because ultimately, I didn't think the people telling me understood where I was coming from. Heck, I was but a youth back then.

I truly believe that young people get tired of hearing parents and teachers talk about how they need to do well. They need to hear it from the people they think are "cool!" Young people need to hear our stories! It is natural for a kid to *only* see the result, the goal, the finished product. It is not so easy to keep in mind the steps required to solidify that goal and make it that much sweeter! Young people need to hear how small the percentage is of players who get paid to play (including overseas) and even if a player is blessed enough to have a professional career, THE BALL WILL STOP BOUNCING SOMEDAY!!

We must let the youth of the world know that being a lifetime learner is indeed very cool! There is nothing better than to see an athlete who is an All-American in their sport, AND an Academic All-American! Students cannot float through school with "eligibility" as their major! And the "not so secret" missing ingredient is when these stellar students hear the perpetual encouragement from people they respect and see themselves being like! John Wooden said it best: "If you don't have time to do it right, when will you have time to do it over?"

Our encouragement to youth cannot be a one-off, *hey make sure you do well in school* either. Our positive affirmation to them must be a consistent, strategic plan to make sure they not only hear it but APPLY it! As most of us know, many times things don't sink in until we get older because the way it is delivered to us is not consistent. I had to go back and get my degree twelve years after I left school, not because I didn't listen, but because I didn't understand exactly what I was hearing. After all, it's easy to forget about the fact you don't have a degree when you are comfortably making money. It is imperative that we not only tell young people how important education is, but also give them a road map to follow in order to get there.

Now that I am retired from pro ball, I find myself asking my friends who are still playing how much longer they will be playing, or what they are going to do when they are done. Amazingly, more times than not, the time left playing is less than three years and the answer to what they are going to do is, "I DON'T KNOW!" Guess what? I fell into that boat too when I was playing. Those surrounding the athlete ask, or may even tell you, "Know what you are going to do after you retire," but that is like telling a young person to drive a car yet failing to tell them how to put the car in gear! There must be a road map that guides young athletes down the path of righteousness because it's certainly not about barking out instructions.

I knew during my basketball career that I wanted to do something in the area of developing and improving players and it still took a year for me to learn how to put my plan into action. It is extremely difficult to transition into work mode after years of playing sports for a living. I watched a Kobe Bryant interview yesterday and even he said he didn't know what he was going to do when his playing years were over. Just as we athletes were encouraged to play each game as if it was our last, we must teach the players of today how to live that way as well. If you wait until you are no longer playing, it is still not too late, but you put yourself behind the eight ball. It is in the learning ourselves that we are equipped to teach our youth how to conduct themselves.

Now, young people, I'm speaking to you! What will you do with the knowledge and experience you have been given? Start applying the knowledge of preparation and how to be ready for anything. Discover what your purpose is and pursue it! I have learned that having a job and having a purpose are two completely different things. Just think if everyone was living their purpose and not merely working a job…the world would be a much happier place because the drudgery of what we think of as the "normal work day" would not exist because people would genuinely love what they were doing.

I'll conclude this chapter by saying, "Young people, let's not only concentrate on doing well in school but know *why* you are doing well in school. As Simon Sinek says in his book, *Start with Why*, "Once you know WHY you do what you do, the question is HOW will you do it?" It is not necessarily to get good grades or a good job. More than that, it is to ensure you understand the process, gain knowledge, evaluate experience and live a fulfilled life over a successful life, and by the way, you CAN do both, but personal fulfillment is the most important.

Trust me, it is a heck of a lot easier (and less expensive) to take care of business when you are a student and not a thirty-five-year-old trying to complete their degree! To my friends who are still living the *playing pro sports dream*, take advantage of all the time you have wherever you are and truly get to know yourself. Read, think, and discover what your purpose is and put a plan into place to help position yourself to live your purpose along with provide for your family when the game is over!

LIVE
EXTRAORDINARY

Dust Yourself Off

This section is dedicated to all the EXTRAordinary Winners. Many of you know I have created an experience called The whY Project. The whY Project is a journey that takes you down the path of learning about yourself and who you truly are, which, in turn, guides you towards your purpose. The whY Project journey comes from an acronym I've created for the word PURPOSE. While I won't discuss the other letters in the acronym at this point, I do want you to know what they are:

> ➤ Passion

> ➤ Uncommon

> ➤ Resilience

> ➤ Preparation

> ➤ Opportunity

> ➤ Service

> ➤ Experience

As you can see, the "R" represents RESILIENCE and for the purpose (no pun intended) of this chapter, and for the purpose of continuing to learn and grow, I did a little research and ran across some interesting information about eaglets that clearly reveals the power of resilience. Let me show you what I mean.

Baby eagles don't go to school like us humans, but they learn an important lesson very early in life. A lesson that all of us would do well to remember. An eaglet's preparation for flight is quite amazing. Young eagles learn how to fly from their parents and by practicing near their nest. One of the main ways they practice is by spreading their wings and jumping to a nearby branch. At first, they hop to the closest branches, flapping their wings and the movement is more like jumping than flying. This exercise helps them improve their coordination and balance. Until the eaglets are able to fly, they depend on their parents for everything. In the nest, the eaglets stretch their wings and hop, gaining strength and balance as they grow.

When it is time for the eaglet to learn to fly, the mother begins to remove the comfort layers from the nest, exposing the pricks and sticks. She then throws the eaglets out of the nest. She does this repeatedly until the eaglet learns to fly. Out of fear, the eaglet jumps back in the nest, with each attempt, shrieking and bleeding from the pricks in the nest. The mother doesn't yield. To others looking on this may seem heartless. But there is a method to her madness. The process is repeated until the eaglet eventually starts flapping its wings, getting stronger and stronger with each flap. Young eagles learn by imitating their parents. Once the young eagles are flying, they still have a lot to learn before they can survive on their own. Watching an adult fly and copying all the moves helps the young birds get it right. Adult eagles are known for their power and ability to fly at high altitudes and can fly where no other bird can fly.

As children, we are often told to soar like an eagle. Aim high and fly. Oh, if only it were that simple! As humans, when we fall and fail, when we are down, sometimes we just give up because there is no one there—no one pushes us out of our comfort zone to remind us that to survive and succeed, we must learn to get back on our feet. Oftentimes we must use the same "eagle" methodology when either we or someone we know has fallen or failed; we need to hand out a couple of pushes of hard truth along with encouragement and positive affirmation so we get back up, tougher and stronger.

I study the lives of high performing people and I see a recurring pattern. Were they always successful in all they did? No. Did success come to them quickly and easily? Absolutely not! When studying high performers, you'll find that the common thread in their lives is their ability to stand up every time they fall. Think mother and baby eagle!

Have you heard about a young girl who dreamt about becoming a teacher or working in radio? She auditioned to break into the TV world. Those in charge felt she wasn't particularly pretty enough and thus she was confined to certain roles and positions. She refused to accept defeat and continued to pursue her dream. Through envisioning a greater future, finding her truth, being a force for good, knowing what she truly wanted, believing in herself, putting out positivity and providing incredible value she caught the attention of a director for a role in a movie. From that movie, the previously limited radio announcer and TV anchor went on to become the world's biggest talk show host. **Her name? Oprah Winfrey.**

The road to greatness is never an easy one. There are so many obstacles and you are bound to fall sooner or later. You'll hit a roadblock, or you'll experience failure of some type, but greatness lies in being able to get up every time you fall. That, my friend, is a critical life skill and it's the habit of all great people.

Learning to win in life is much like a baby learning to walk. As they begin to walk, they will fall and get frustrated and sometimes cry, but all that doesn't matter. Babies learn to get back up and continue to improve. Fall one more time? Get back up one more time. Simple, but not easy. You must learn to get back up every time you fall.

What would happen if parents constantly hovered over their baby and never let them fall? That baby would never learn to walk...and run.

One more thing. Next time you feel like a friend or a parent is pushing you, don't get upset with them. Like the mother eagle, they may simply be teaching you one of life's most important lessons. It doesn't matter how many times you fall. What matters is your ability to dust yourself off and stand on your feet once again.

I QUIT

"Winners never quit and quitters never win." We've all heard that phrase in some way, shape or form. I ask you, should we take that phrase literally, or are there situations where quitting is okay? In this chapter we're going to talk about quitting and how we can incorporate not quitting AND quitting into our lives.

As a society, we've turned quitting into a curse word with phrases like "Quitting is for losers" and "It's always too soon to quit" credited to Norman Vincent Peale, and then there's Idowu Koyenikan's quote, "If you quit on the process, you are quitting on the result." I'm here to tell you that **quitting can be the positive process of choosing the path that more fully serves your highest calling.** Read that sentence again and really allow it to sink into your soul. Don't get caught up in the lie of "I can't end that course of action because then I'll be a quitter." Instead, you should ask yourself, *does this action serve what's truly best for my wellbeing?* When it does, give no apologies for following that path.

For many high school basketball players across the country, try-outs officially start every fall. Some of them enter the gym KNOWING they either are or are not going to make the team. Another group of them walk in with the mentality of doing well enough to give themselves a legitimate shot of making it. And then there is the last group of athletes, the ones that couldn't care less if they make the team or not. Why? Because they have no interest in playing the sport anymore but cling on for some reason. That reason could be their friends who still play and have a love for the game, it could be because their parents want them to play, or it could be because they've always played and the uncertainty of not playing is so scary that they would rather be unhappy than uncertain. These reasons are legitimate reasons but should never be considered the ultimate factors in the decision-making process because of the fear of being labelled a quitter.

So, when is quitting a good thing? There are lots of reasons to quit:

Quit the job you hate.

Quit the relationship that isn't serving you.

Quit the friendships that are draining.

Quit the tasks that are sucking the soul right out of you.

Quit the habit that is weakening your health.

I'm not sure exactly when we were taught that "quitters never prosper" or "quitters never win, and winners never quit." I'm also not sure why we were taught that there is honor in finishing things that are unfulfilling, toxic or stressful. The message has been *you'll win if you don't quit.*

Here's the danger in being fearful of quitting. You can get stuck. Instead of focusing on what is important to you, what makes you feel happy, healthy and free, your primary focus becomes not quitting. You stop being strategic. You stop thinking about whether your decisions will lead you to the life you want to live. You stop thinking about YOU!!! Being "selfish" has such a negative connotation in today's world that everyone goes out of their way to make sure they don't fall into that category. But looking after yourself and making sure you are taken care of is not being negatively selfish, it's showing self-love. The problem happens when you care *only* about yourself with a disregard for other people. THAT'S when it becomes negative.

Quitting isn't the problem. Quitting is a very necessary part of life. Individuals make so many decisions in their lives, and those decisions are driven by one factor—not wanting to quit in order to save face. They don't want to be perceived as a failure. People have such a fear of failing that they steer clear of anything that looks or smells like failure. So, we stay in unhealthy relationships because we want to fight through and make it work; because we don't want to fail. We stay in toxic friendships because we don't want to cut it off. We want to figure it out, work it out, and make it work at all costs to our personal happiness and well-being. We suppress the stress, the pain, the tears, just to push through. All to avoid looking like a "failure."

What we don't realize is by not quitting, we are failing. We fail to put ourselves first. We fail to follow our dreams. We fail at having enough confidence to walk our own path. As I've said, there is a difference between necessary and unnecessary quitting. Sometimes, quitting is necessary. If we are talking about an unhealthy addiction like drugs, alcohol, or gambling, we'd all agree that someone should work on quitting to break those bad habits, but we often neglect to think about less blatant bad habits we need to let go. Unhealthy relationships with food. Unfulfilling jobs. Toxic relationships. All these things lead to stress, and stress wreaks havoc on the mind and body. We must take care of ourselves and sometimes that means knowing when to call it quits.

When you find yourself in a stressful situation, remember it's *All About the whY*. Ask yourself, why am I doing this? Why do I want to quit? WhY questions are important because they automatically make you think about why you continue in that situation. Does the situation bring you joy, or does it put you on a path of misery and depression?

Think for a moment about what joy means to you. Do you expect joy in your everyday life, with the people you interact with daily? You should! Sure, we have to muscle through some tough life circumstances, and we must persevere through relationship issues so I'm not saying to quit at the first sign of distress. Therefore, you need to make sure that you aren't just facing a challenge you need to push through. If you want to change your physical appearance, you are going to experience moments of intense cravings when you want to eat that large pile of nachos instead of hitting the gym. When you set a goal of running a mile, keep going! Don't just quit because you are tired.

What I'm saying is to know when to quit and when to persevere.

An athlete recently approached me to have a sincere, genuine conversation. Bottom line: he didn't want to pursue basketball at a competitive level anymore but didn't know how to tell his dad because he feared his dad's reaction. This young man was so fearful of his dad's reaction that he chose to put stress, anguish and anxiety on himself just to keep his dad happy. I told him what my "Big Mama" used to tell me. "Pray on it, you don't have the words to say, but God does." I continued, "Your dad may be upset initially but in the long run he will respect you for being open and honest, and you will be in a much better place mentally and physically with that load off your chest."

Please understand this: hard work is a must. You shouldn't quit things just because they are hard or challenging. But, if you realize that you do not want to play basketball because you are passionate about art, then quitting may be the absolute right thing to do. Only you will know if you are being strategic or lazy. You must be honest with yourself.

Next, ask yourself how the situation or person makes you feel. If the thought of doing a task or seeing a certain person brings on intense anxiety or makes you feel physically ill, it's probably time to re-evaluate the situation.

When you're playing sports at any level, every day will not be a cake walk nor will you experience extreme feelings of happiness, but your situation shouldn't be causing you mental and physical stress. If you aren't passionate about sports, your job, or your relationship, and you're still engaging because it sounds good or someone else expects you to, the stress is NOT worth it. Again, only *you* can decide the right path.

Sometimes quitting is the right answer and sometimes it is not. Sometimes you need to be resilient and sometimes you need to let go. You may need grit, or you may need compassion. The goal is harmony. The goal is to figure out the appropriate time for each response. Perhaps it is time to follow the advice of Kenny Rogers: "You got to know when to hold 'em, know when to fold 'em, know when to walk away, know when to run..."

Mo' Money. Mo' Problems.

"Mo' Money, Mo' Problems," sings Notorious B.I.G.

Recently, I've been reading a lot of financial books: Dave Ramsey, Robert Kiyosaki, Tony Robbins, to name a few. The funny thing is although they have some fundamental differences in action steps, all the material basically boils down to the same thing…as a society we are AWFUL at managing money!

Let me speak from personal experience first. Growing up, there was no talk about money in my house unless it was about how little we had. My father was my superman; he taught me so much about love, the importance of family and respect for myself as well as others. However, he was not able to teach me how to understand money, be financially responsible, and how to make money work for me! Through learning and experience I have discovered that this lack of financial education has no zip code, no color, and it doesn't matter if the previous generation was financially well off.

The average professional athlete is a first-generation pro which means he is a first generation "money-aire." I use that word because it doesn't take millions to make you think you're rich if you've been used to living off $15-20k per year! A first generation "money-aire" usually has no clue how money works because they have never had much of it to deal with, so I ask you, how can they take the blame when they have been forced to live check to check even though they now make $15-20k *per month* instead of per year? There are always those who are happy to dole out advice and opinions on what should be happening with a young pro athlete's money, but directions ARE NOT the same as DIRECTION.

It is so easy for new pro players to get caught up in impressing their so-called friends with the possessions they have access to with their newfound riches. And I don't care what anyone says; you ALWAYS want to show off a little bit, it's human nature. Showing off a little bit is not the problem. The problem lies when showing off becomes a lifestyle! Let me give you an example.

The overseas basketball market has drastically gone down over the past few years because the world financial crisis has affected the global corporate markets, the direct sponsors of professional teams of all sports. I personally know people who have $500k homes or $90k cars they can't pay for because their $350k job they had four years ago is now paying $125k. While $125k sounds fantastic to the average person, when a pro athlete's monthly expenses (that "friends" have become accustomed to) are over $10,000 per month, $125k doesn't quite get it done. See what I mean now?

American society is a "get more, buy more" society where the emphasis is on how much you *appear* to have. Here's a quick nugget of knowledge: the IRS absolutely LOVES the American athlete because the more material things we buy, the more we must show the government how much money we make. It's all about taxable income which means now the IRS makes a profit on taxes paid! I know athletes and entertainers who have two Bentleys, four Benzes, a Rolls Royce and a Lamborghini in the driveway. We must act smarter with our money! Athletes: don't live *within* your means, learn how to live *below* your means, and surround yourself with people who have knowledge and your best interest in mind when it comes to financial decisions. Educate yourself on how to eliminate working *for* your money—have your money work for you!

The people in charge who you are "ballin" for will be the same ones calling you stupid at the end of your career and asking you what you did with all that money. We trick ourselves into justifying our foolish decisions by thinking we are doing what people expect a "baller" to do or emulating how we believe a "baller" is supposed to look. Many people who surround you know that a baller is supposed to invest their money and prepare for the day their checks stop rolling in, but again, this is not something we are trained to think when we are playing and collecting hefty checks every month. When we're playing, we know next month that check will be there just like it was the month before. You would be amazed how long it took me to understand that on a typical overseas contract of nine months that the most difficult months were the three months I wasn't getting paid. All withdrawals with no deposits are not good for anyone's account!

Please don't misunderstand me by thinking I am saying not to enjoy your money and treat yourself. I love shoes and will always want a new pair; that's just me. What I *am* saying is understand how money works and understand how credit works. Credit does not just come in plastic form. You will have a very difficult time beating financial people at the money game just as they would not fare well against you on the court or field. Learn the money game! Learn to live by, "If you can't pay cash for something, you don't need it!" I guarantee your material indulgences will drastically reduce. The Bible says in Proverbs 22:7 that the rich rule over the poor and the borrower is slave to the lender!

The Things We Know But Do Not Do

I've learned a few very important lessons about money I'd like to share with you:

1. Money truly is like a ride at the amusement park; however, it is up to you whether the ride is the Big Dipper or just bumper cars.

2. Many of us will walk past the average millionaire not knowing it because he or she will not be draped in diamonds or driving a Phantom. They won't be in a pair of $300 jeans or have a ridiculous mortgage. They will likely be in a used car, wearing a pair of Levi's, quietly going to the mailbox and depositing money into their account to go on vacation with their family!

3. I have learned there is a huge difference between being rich and being wealthy. Chris Rock said it well: "Shaq is rich…the person who writes Shaq's check is wealthy!" My all-time favorite line though is from Andre 3000 who states, "Rich ain't nothing but around the corner from the curb!" I have been rich and the only thing I learned from being rich is how close the curb really is!

Jayson Wells

Simple Versus Easy

Is it simple, or is it easy? Let's put it this way; there are a lot of things that are simple, but aren't in the least bit easy.

Let's start with simple. If I were to ask you, "What do I need to do to get more fit?" Everyone knows the answer; proper diet and fitness routines done with discipline and consistency. Simple, but not easy. Inevitably, the day you start your steps towards your fitness goals, your friends will call and say let's go watch the game and have some pizza or they'll invite you to the new dessert place that has amazing red velvet cupcakes. Now, because of the game and the sweets, you get home late, and when the alarm goes off at six a.m. the next morning and you know you need to work out, you hit snooze until it's too late and now it's time for work or school. After work, time gets crazy and... I believe you get the picture. Simple is NOT easy.

There are numerous examples I can use to discuss the differences between simple and easy. The fact remains that simple and easy are not synonyms. The simple thing to do is often NOT the easy thing to do.

I have conversations all the time about what I do in my basketball workouts. My workouts are designed around SIMPLICITY; things you can learn, perform and then put them directly into your game. I don't care if you can dribble between your legs, cross, behind, or step back—your defender is still standing right in front of you. I don't care if you can juggle a tennis ball blindfolded while you dribble. I don't even care if you can dribble two basketballs at one time. My coach used to always tell us, "I ain't never played or coached a game where two basketballs were on the court!" Believe me, I totally

46

The Things We Know But Do Not Do

understand that for dexterity, concentration and coordination, the abovementioned things can enhance those three skills. I find that parents often question me about my philosophy because I don't use two balls to dribble or enlist other "trick" type practice techniques. I tell them, "I can't juggle tennis balls or shoot a jumper with both hands, but I got paid to play this game for thirteen years because my game was versatile and efficient."

More inspiration on this topic came from a longtime friend who is a high school teacher. She is struggling with the overall demeanor and behavior of the students in her school. In our conversation, she mentioned their language when interacting with others, even in the presence of a teacher or administrator. She believes this conduct comes from the information and input students are receiving from music, movies and other media outlets. My response to her was "meet them where they are." So often, when we're tasked with the development of people, especially young people, we get frustrated because we want them to be in a place they aren't ready for. Instead, meet them where they are. Simple, but not easy. We ended our conversation with the idea of researching current celebrities that teenagers are listening to or watching and finding short, one- to two-minute blurbs of those celebrities speaking about something positive in an interview or video clip. People teens are interested in, delivering short but meaningful information, will change teens' perspective of receiving positive information. Once you have them engaged with the consistency of receiving positive information, you move on to other people outside their comfort zone with longer, even more impactful videos. Simple, but not easy.

I did a little research and here's how scholars differentiated the words "simple" and "easy."

Definitions of "Simple"

- Simple can mean that something is easy. Ex: "2 + 2 = 4 is a very simple bit of math."

- Something that is basic or fundamental is also simple. "It's a simple truth: falling and missing the ground is impossible."

- Simple can also be used to show that something isn't complicated or fancy. "She wore a simple black dress."

Definitions of "Easy"

- An easy thing is one that is not difficult to do. "It was easy to walk up the hill."

- An easy life is laid back and free of worry. "I want the easy life of someone who inherited a million dollars."

- It could mean that someone is free of awkwardness. "He won them over with his easy charm," or "Her easy manner made her popular."

As you can see, the two are similar but not quite the same. I have developed my own personal vision of simple and easy. Easy is often fun, convenient and entertaining. Simple means conquering boredom, mastering the fundamentals and becoming an expert in greatness through repetition. There are times when "simple" and "easy" are interchangeable, but there are times when they aren't. It all depends on context. Your views on "simple" versus "easy" may differ from mine. Different doesn't mean right or wrong, it's just different, and I embrace that.

The Reality of a Dream

In this chapter I'm going to explore the difference between **reality** and **dreaming**, and why some athletes struggle with those concepts when it comes to hanging it up.

Basketball has basically been my life for over thirty years. From the age of three when I picked up my first ball, to seventh grade when I played on my first organized team, basketball was it! I had no idea my dream of getting paid to play a game I loved would allow me to see places in the world I didn't even know existed! Basketball has allowed me to be in the same city as three Olympic Ceremonies (Atlanta, Sydney, and Athens). It has allowed me to live in, NOT VISIT, the Holy Land of Israel, not to mention that my oldest son was born in Italy. I've had the opportunity to cross paths with some of the most wonderful people on the planet. I've also had the opportunity to financially benefit from my skillset.

For thirteen seasons I woke up every morning and was able to say, "I am a professional basketball player!" You may think that my first day of waking up and not being able to say that would make reality set in quickly. NO WAY!! Over eight years after I officially decided that I had played my last game, reality was finally setting in that my life was NOT playing basketball anymore. I had no idea how to stop dreaming and face my new reality! After years of being able to do exactly what they want—play ball—many players simply do not know how to wake up to any other reality. Whether it's hanging on too long, retiring and then coming back, or simply trying to make a couple more bucks, it happens entirely too often. I believe most athletes, many of whom have made millions of dollars, are quite simply...scared! Scared of "real life," scared of what the world holds outside of putting a ball through a hoop. And though my background is basketball, please don't be fooled into believing that it only happens in my sport! Guys like Mike Tyson and Paul Pierce succumb to the harsh reality of their new life outside their sport. And all of us remember watching Brett Favre unravel right in front of our eyes. The truly sad part is that the story never ends well. When you pass on your opportunity to leave the game gracefully, you will not have that option again; from that point on your only option is to get KNOCKED OUT!!

Imagine this: You are the best basketball player on the planet, nobody argues it, your team is down one point in the championship series, and everyone knows this game could be the last time they ever see you play. 8, 7, 6, 5, shot... IT'S GOOD!!! The crowd goes wild, the announcers are shrieking, "Can you believe that?" You leave the follow-through up so the whole world can see the "trophy form" as that shot will all but secure a third straight championship for the second time in your career and conclude the best professional career of any player EVER! With that final play, you get to leave on top, I mean really on top. Who wouldn't want their career to end like that? Try the guy that it happened to! Anyone who knows me knows Michael Jordan is my all-time favorite player, hands down, no questions asked. But because he could not "wake up," my last vision of him was on the court as a slow, less athletic guy in a WASHINGTON WIZARDS uniform! Brett Favre, MJ, Allen Iverson; playing in Turkey, guys still hanging on to a crappy job in a crappy market halfway across the world are all examples of guys in an athletic coma who refuse to wake up. It's unfortunate I have to say this, but in all actuality, each case of the players mentioned above playing past their prime is the result of a self-induced coma, because forcing themselves to continue playing in their comfort zone was a heck of a lot less frightening than the uncertainty of the unknown!

I believe the following statements express the top reasons we find athletes in an athletic coma:

1. "I have no idea what I'm going to do once the dream is over!"

2. "I'm not going to be able to do what I want to do because I didn't get my degree."

3. "I have lived such a baller's life that I have to keep playing to try to maintain the lifestyle that everyone around me has become accustomed to."

4. "I have nothing to show for the work I put in because my bank account shows I may as well have been unemployed for the last two years because nobody actually showed me how to handle my money."

When an athlete of any age has been through the athletic coma battle, it's much like any other learning experience the rest of humanity goes through, especially our youth of today. Often the best thing to do is to take time to talk, teach and support the next generation, athletes and non-athletes alike, so they don't have to keep making the same mistakes! It also requires the next generation to be willing to listen, learn and apply the knowledge they receive so they can grow and pass more on to the group after them.

I've heard so much talk lately about how "messed up" this generation is, and I too believe that they DO have challenges! However, I have made a commitment to myself and to them to make a change—I refuse to sit and complain about it, I will actively influence, impact and inspire. At some point, we must stop blaming the apples and put some responsibility on the TREE.

You Big Dummy!

This chapter's title is inspired by one of my favorite childhood TV characters, Fred Sanford from the show *Sanford and Son*. "You big dummy" was one of Fred's classic lines he was always telling his son, Lamont. Keep the title of this chapter in mind as I discuss personal development and why it is such a hit or miss topic.

I'm sure most everyone reading this book is aware of what personal development is, but just in case you need a refresher, it is simply, "activities that improve awareness, and develop talents and potential within an individual." But here's my question: By the description you just read, why isn't EVERYONE on a constant and ongoing pursuit of personal development? I believe there are three main reasons.

1. **IT'S NOT ENCOURAGED** – I am speaking primarily about the workplace with this one. I've found that *some* industries and *some* companies place a high value on personal development, but it's still kind of dependent on whether the leaders of that industry or company place a high value on it, and not because there is a burning desire to have it implemented. Let's face it, if your CEO tells you that you must go to a seminar or conference, you're going to have to go but in contrast I bet you'd have a harder time getting time off if you asked your CEO if you can take two days to go to a personal development conference to learn, grow and improve. The second part should be happening way more often than it does but employers are still resistant to simply hand out days off so their employees can improve themselves, which ironically will most often improve their productivity at work.

2. **SELFISHNESS** – The culture we live in nowadays has placed such a negative connotation on the word "selfish" that I believe we have lost the true meaning and essence of the healthy benefits of being selfish. The act of loving yourself, believing in yourself and improving yourself IS NOT SELFISH! It's when you do those things at the expense of other people that it becomes negative selfishness. I believe there are more people than would care to admit it who don't pursue personal development because they don't want to appear selfish in the eyes of others—they believe other people will think, *who do they think they are, doing all this improvement stuff?*

3. **I DON'T HAVE ENOUGH TIME** – For the sake of my PG-13 audience, I'm just gonna say "NONSENSE!!" That excuse is the biggest bunch of crap ever! You have time for anything you want to do, you just choose to prioritize other things ahead of personal development. You need some examples? What about these: "I just don't have time to sit down and read… But you have time to watch Walking Dead, Game of Thrones, or some UNreality TV show? Or how about this one: "By the time my day is over, I'm just too tired." You know, I get asked all the time WHY I wake up at 4:30 A.M. It's because I have consciously worked time into my day to dedicate towards personal development! I call the time between 5:00-7:00 A.M. my "PRIME TIME" where I work out, read, stretch, meditate, and watch videos. I choose the beginning of the day because I feel like it helps me start my day off right. Either way, you HAVE time. There are audio podcasts and audiobooks for the car ride instead of that favorite jam you've heard five hundred and twenty-one times…you know…that one tune where you know all the words, breaths and pauses. You've just chosen your priority and that's cool. My friend and business coach told me a couple years ago,

"I'm never mad at what someone else chooses to prioritize, but they can't be mad at me for being further ahead."

In conclusion, personal development is a MUST for ALL OF US! MAKE the time to get better. It's not selfish and you should be doing it whether an employer tells you to or not. Personal development is for YOU and it's the most loving thing you can do for those who surround you because as you become a better person, your newfound excellence will rub off on those around you, and your new habits will positively affect those around you. Remember, at the end of the day, if I get better and you get getter, then WE get better.

ELEVATE YOUR GAME

Until Death Do Us Part

I remember summers in Cleveland, Ohio. I was always at least a year younger than all my classmates and friends so playing with the older "big" boys was nothing new, and it taught me how to be tough, strong-minded and how to overcome physical challenges. By the time I got to Cleveland Central Catholic High School as a thirteen-year-old freshman, I was ready for anything thrown at me because my neighborhood ball playing prepared me. For the first three years of high school, my play on the basketball court was rather ordinary. Then, a growth spurt...and I mean a spurt!

Leaving school for the summer in May of my junior year I was sixteen and five feet eleven inches. Coming back in August, I was six feet six inches! Playing with guys like Earl Boykins, Javier Smith and Barney James, there were always college coaches at our games. They came looking at Earl or Javier, but they left asking who the tall, skinny kid was. Nothing really materialized until I was selected to play in the Greater Cleveland Coaches Classic. Sherman Dillard had just been hired at Indiana State University; he saw me and invited me to visit campus. Coach Dillard's offer was my only sincere scholarship offer and no way was I going to college without a scholarship, so my decision was made. Terre Haute, Indiana, here I come!!

Those first few weeks of college were like nothing I had ever experienced to that point. Now a seventeen-year-old freshman, away from home for the first time ever, I had no idea what to do. 6am conditioning, open team runs in the afternoon, and class in between. I often asked myself, "What did I sign up for?" The other freshman I came in with, Derrick Stroud, was from Griffin, Georgia. He was about my height, about my size, but man I couldn't stop this guy for anything! I remember hearing one upperclassman say, "I don't know what they saw in him." I was weak and slow, the game seemed to move so fast, I was always a step late and a dollar short. Six feet six inches and one hundred seventy-one pounds is what the freshman year media guide said next to my name. I spent that year getting stronger physically while I practiced daily against guys who were up to seven years older than me. I went from sitting on the bench my freshman year to starting as a sophomore! I received the Top 3-Point Shooter award in the conference my sophomore season, then 3rd team All-Conference my junior year, but the breakthrough came senior year. Coach Dillard left to go back to his alma mater and in came a new coaching staff led by a "Bobby Knight disciple!"

Royce Waltman, a short, white-haired guy with a temper that would scare a grizzly bear and a coaching style to match! But man, this guy just flat out knew the game. The first thing he did after watching us play during pre-season was establish roles on the team. "You, you and you, can shoot threes whenever you want. You and you can shoot them when you're open and the rest of you, if you even stop at the three-point line, you're coming out!" That was a typical example of his style. But I tell you what, you learned to accept your role and play, or sit on the bench. That was really my first experience with a coach who embraced and lived his style and his philosophy, and you either bought in or you didn't! We ended up having ISU's first winning season since the year after Larry Bird left and individually, we had three All-Conference selections led by yours truly on the All Conference 1st team!

After playing my way into a professional job that I have no shame in saying paid me $30k, I was blessed to have much of my thirteen-year professional career surrounded by great guys and decent coaches. I had teammates who had enough respect for themselves and for me, to critique and to be critiqued. I had coaches who taught and disciplined players, no matter whether they were a starter or a junior player who wasn't going to see the court. There was integrity in the game, respect for the game, and respect for each other. I grew up (both as a kid and as a pro) being taught if your teammate had a better shot, pass it and let him take that shot, that if a good screen led to a great shot, the screen was just as good as the shot, and younger players instinctively listened to older players because they yearned for knowledge and experience that would make them better.

Fast forward to the present day. The reason I made note of my first job's salary is because many of today's players would not be willing to admit that they might not be good enough to demand a $75k job, or that taking a $30k job is better than most people do on their first job outside of sports. For many of today's players, it's all about the now, not about the process, not about working hard, not about showing you deserve a raise! Everything I was taught as a young player is non-existent these days. The game today reeks of a "me first" mentality. If the team loses, but "I" scored 30, I did my job. Or it's "who cares about the fact it took me thirty-five shots to get to thirty-five points, I got my thirty-five points!" The game today is filled with young guys who catch feelings when they are critiqued by older players, and I mean real feelings...like they won't talk to you until Saturday over something that was said Tuesday! And for heaven's sake don't let one of the stars have a problem with the coach because sooner or later that coach will be packing his bags. Can you imagine Magic Johnson bumping into Pat Riley walking into a timeout? Weak coaches today will hold their criticism of a star player to make sure he doesn't ruffle that player's feathers, or worse yet, a coach will yell at another player, knowing his anger should have been directed at Mr. Star Player.

The game I love has changed, which is why I decided to call it quits. I was tired of being labeled "not aggressive" because I wasn't out there chucking up shots like the rest of my teammates. I was tired of having my teammates mad at me because I was telling them the things coach should have been telling them. I was tired of having to bottle up my emotions on the BS that went on earlier in the day. So, for anyone wondering why I stopped when I still had "gas in the tank," it's because I was not going to keep stressing myself physically and mentally to change things that I couldn't change. Early in my career there were ten guys with a common goal which made it easy to eliminate the two who may have had their own agenda. Now, there are ten guys with their own agenda and the two guys with a common goal are the ones who are eliminated! What's wrong with that picture?! So, I made the decision to do what I can do, and that is develop young players and teach them the values and principles I was taught—principles that are learned on the basketball court yet seamlessly transferred off the court. Values like work ethic, attitude, passion, competition, punctuality and spirit. I experience just as much joy now as I did when I was running up and down the court. The new catch phrase is "trust the process." Well, I have no choice but to "trust the process," because I AM THE PROCESS! At the end of the day, I will not abandon the game I love because when I fell in love it was until death do us part.

Five Reasons Why Your Kid Sucks

Did the title of this chapter grab your attention? I hope so! I know you probably don't want to hear this but you're like every other parent in the world…and I mean the world! I've gone to Belgium for the past couple of years and I quickly learned that parents also think the same way there as in the United States. Whether abroad or here in the States, nine times out of ten I bet I can read your thoughts: "My child is better than the kid who gets all the playing time…why is that?" Well, let's dive into the deep end. I'm going to give you some honest, unbiased clarity. Here are my top five reasons why your child doesn't get the playing minutes you think they deserve.

1. **Academics** – Let's be completely honest and upfront here. If this isn't first on the top of you and your child's priority list, then why even discuss reasons two through five? Sadly, there are still way too many cases where a player shoots themselves in the foot before they even touch the playing surface. Each team, school, state association, and collegiate organization has some form of academic requirements, that if they aren't met will automatically eliminate any player from competing. This is a no brainer! Get it together!

2. **Attitude** – So many times "having a bad attitude" is misunderstood. We all know what a "bad attitude" looks like, right? The player who gets subbed out of the game and immediately goes to the end of the bench to pout and complain about why they got taken out. Or, how about the player who just knows he's better than everybody else on the team and acts like a total idiot to prove it? He talks down to his teammates and acts like he is the reason the game was invented. These are clear cases of not-so-great attitudes. But your child doesn't act like that, right?

What about the less obvious "bad attitudes?" What about the players who create conflict throughout the team in subliminal ways, like secretly talking about coach and how bad he or she is (most often stemming from a conversation that started at home), or the player who just doesn't work as hard as they should? Honestly assess these attitudes with your child and see if they are applicable.

3. **Ability** – Your child has good grades and a good attitude and still isn't playing. Let me explain it to you this way: If your student-athlete has good grades and a good attitude, chances are, you need to consider their ability. This is very difficult because now we start to dig into areas that require some serious truth sessions. Hey, it's okay! Every player isn't going to have the physical talent to be the star or even a background star. But clearly, coach thought your child brought something to the team they desired, otherwise they would've been cut! Instead of fighting the system and questioning the coach's every decision, how about embracing your child's role while consistently speaking about how they should be developing their leadership qualities? Believe me, it will ease tension all the way around.

4. **THEM** – Too many times, we well-meaning adults never really take into consideration our own child's mentality and mindset. We are too busy supporting, encouraging, cheering on, or complaining, so we get lost in our emotions and forget about theirs. Maybe your child has no real desire to play a lot of minutes in a game. Maybe your child just wants the camaraderie of being around their friends on the team. Or, maybe your child doesn't truly understand what it takes to get better. If that's truly what they want, then embrace their goal and help them understand that getting better requires daily, purposeful improvement.

And remember, you can't beat it into them because they'll just resist and resent you. Show them what it takes in a supportive, encouraging way and let them enjoy the ride!

5. **YOU** – I saved the best for last, and this, by far, is the most important reason—it's YOU! I've seen parents of all ages, ethnicities, social demographics, and genders *be* the reason their child isn't playing like they think they should. First things first, THIS IS YOUR CHILD'S ATHLETIC CAREER, NOT YOURS! Geez, if I see another parent live vicariously through their child, I'm gonna lose it! As I said before, you cannot force your child to love the game like you do or work as hard as you worked. That approach is much more destructive than helpful. Let your child live. Talk to them, listen to them, show them what hard work looks like from a place of love and support instead of yelling and questioning why they just don't get it. WINNING IS NOT EVERYTHING, especially before high school. No one cares if your child won the fifth-grade championship once they enter high school. Concentrate on overall development not winning! There is a stat that says seventy percent of young athletes who start sports at age six quit by age thirteen! Why? YOU! "The ride home." The questions you ask. The statements you make. When you say those things, your child's mentality becomes making sure they don't disappoint you rather than what it should be, HAVE FUN, LEARN and GROW! Here's the shocking part; from my experience it's Mom who usually falls into this category. Dad, you don't get off the hook though, because we all know you can be over the top as well. And if you're reading this, thinking quietly to yourself, "He's not talking about me," you Are EXACTLY who I'm talking about! Take a step back, be a parent, love your child for who they are, not who YOU want them to be!

Grades and attitude are usually easy to understand and apply. Ability, understanding your child's objectives, and looking in the mirror at yourself are the more difficult areas. All it takes though is some honesty, maturity and looking at the big picture. Someone asked me recently, "What breaks your heart?" My answer was very clear. "What breaks my heart is the fact that we have created such a pressure- and tension-filled environment throughout youth athletics that we are making young athletes hate the game before they ever get a chance to love it!" Let your child fall in love with the game the way I did—organically, by having fun and seeing the fruit of hard work pay off, by developing confidence along the way because I saw myself improving. We are tearing down our young people with something that is supposed to be fun and enjoyable. It's on us to do better!

Wake Up!

I got the title for this chapter from Spike Lee's movie, *School Daze*, when Laurence Fishburne's character continuously rang the bell on campus urging his fellow students to WAAAAAAAAKE UUUUP! We need that same kind of bell for today's sports scene.

Elite teams, national rankings, and how many games you can play in front of college coaches has evolved from a thing of excitement to a thing of disgust! We, yes, WE have created and enabled a mindset and mentality within the youth basketball culture that shouts, "If my child doesn't play on an elite team in one organization, I will move them around until I find an organization that accommodates my desire." Why? I'm going to call it how I see it. Because doing so validates YOUR ego! You believe that your relentless demonstration of pursuit shows everyone what an awesome parent you are! You believe, *Hey, everyone, look! My kids plays on this team, look how good they are, which obviously means I'm a great parent!*

NEWSFLASH…If your child is good enough to be on an "elite" team, YOU WON'T HAVE TO SHOP THEM AROUND!!! Those teams will FIND your child! I hope what I just said serves as an ah-ha moment for some of you reading this.

We are so caught up in the name and title of the team our children play for that we have put the important things on the back burner. "What important things?" you might ask. Things like the sports organization's philosophy on character development. The organization's philosophy on developing your child's game so they continue to improve. The organization's philosophy on making sure your child's grades stay above average so they can qualify for the scholarship you're pursuing.

Rankings, rankings, rankings! For those of you who know me personally, you know that I keep my hair short and rankings are one of the reasons why. I would be bald or have all gray hair because of these doggone rankings! As a high school junior or senior, to know where you rank nationally against your peers is one thing. It's a whole different thing to be a fifth or sixth grader worried about some national ranking! The other day my friend sent me a text with "#1 player in the class of 2028!" To spare you the math, that's a third-grade child who is roughly eight years old. You should be ashamed of yourself if that is your mentality! I have a nine-year-old son and if someone came up to me talking about he was nationally ranked at anything, they may not even get the statement out before we go to blows. Do you realize how much development, growth and maturity happens between ages nine and sixteen? The child who is ranked highly at age nine probably won't even be on anyone's radar by age sixteen.

Imagine what happens to a child's mentality when they've been nationally ranked since they were six. It's no wonder this generation feels so entitled. Picture what early ranking does to a child's parents—it gives them a false sense of promise that *someone* said your child was a good athlete at age nine means that's going to translate into a college scholarship in another seven years. What a joke! The only thing that is guaranteed to happen to a child in the third grade who is nationally ranked is they're going to go to fourth grade!

Attention parents! Think about whom you're putting your trust in. Many of the guys doing these rankings have NO playing experience and NO coaching experience. So, you are essentially putting your child's future into the hands of someone whose only knowledge of the game is the books they've read and videos they've watched!

Now don't get me wrong, there are some GREAT evaluators out there, like my guys Scott Burgess or Wes Hinton, and these guys know how I feel about the subject of ranking and they also know they aren't a part of what I'm going to say next. Now I'm speaking to all the lowlifes who are exploiting young athletes, their families, and the game I love—I hope you read this and exit the premises IMMEDIATELY!

Parents, let your children fall in love with the game. Put them in situations and surround them with great people and great coaches who will teach them life lessons while they learn their sport. Allow your kids to make mistakes and let them come up short sometimes because those lessons are much more important than winning every game. Put your kids on teams that have a diverse makeup so they can see what the world really looks like. Focus on the total development of your child; personal development, character development and leadership development so WHEN the ball stops bouncing, they are well rounded individuals who will contribute to society.

And children...enjoy your childhood! Be nine years old and don't rush to be eighteen. It will come soon enough. Make mistakes at fifteen and learn from them so hopefully you don't make them again at twenty-five. Enjoy being around your friends—I have guys who I've known all my life because of this game of basketball. And most of all, stop working so hard at getting seen and work more at getting GOOD. In the next chapter, let's fall in love with basketball again, the way it was meant to be played!

For the Love of the Game

I was introduced to the game of basketball when I was three years old. I realized very early that basketball would be my first love. It didn't matter if it was Thursday night Nerf hoop battles at my Big Mama's house or dodging potholes and gravel at Bizbee (my local playground) with friends, I knew basketball was it! MJ said it best when he said, "God must have thought to himself, I better make a ball player outta him, 'cuz if he has to work, this kid will starve!" No man or woman could have taught me the lessons I've learned through playing basketball. And for that, I am forever in love with the game it used to be.

You might be thinking, so what's wrong? What's the problem? The game of basketball is still around but it's not the game I was taught. The game I watch and read about now shows a bunch of guys who can run fast, jump high and shoot so many threes that some are bound to go in. Many of these kids have no idea what the basketball IQ side of the game is, or what it's truly like to work your tail off to get better. Somebody has told him how great a player he is since he was five, all because he could dribble! From then on, every coach he's had from summer ball through high school has done nothing but set him up for lobs and has yelled "take him" from the bench, dribbling the air out of the ball trying to go one on one. Now, his college coach (who used to be a youth player's last chance to develop) is forced to basically teach this kid how to play the game. That is if coach even has enough time, because he knows that kid is only staying one year before he goes and makes all his dreams come true!

So where does the breakdown start with my disappointment in our youth coaches? Across the board, many of them are not teaching the game, heck most of them don't even really know the game to be able to teach it! Many youth coaches are dads who may have played in high school, basically living their hoop dreams out through these kids. Don't get me wrong, I love dads for being there and getting involved in young people's lives, especially given the state we are in nowadays with the lack of positive male role models, but at some point, basketball and the nuances of the game must be taught. That's not going to happen by just rolling the balls out and letting a team scrimmage. Parents need to take a serious look at how they're approaching the game.

Today's parent is so falsely involved that they are corrupting the kids before they even get a chance to experience the game for themselves. Examples include Mom thinking that because somebody told her how good her son was, she has the right to threaten his high school coach with transferring if the team doesn't revolve around her son. Or, Mom and Dad having the kid believe NOTHING is his fault, his grades aren't his fault, coach "picking on you" is not his fault. LET'S BE SERIOUS! I realize that Bobby Knight's method of coaching is non-existent, but c'mon—teach the kids *some* accountability. Tell him the reason he's getting "picked on" is because coach believes he is not doing his best and expects more out of him! Believe me, little Johnny won't die. In fact, it might make him try harder, play better, and get stronger.

Most parents and players today think they are the next LeBron or KD; the next superstar NBA player! NOT!! Those guys are great players who have God-given talent, mixed with extraordinary work ethic! Kobe Bryant, love him or hate him, was the hardest working guy in the game. He spent his off seasons eliminating weaknesses and improving his skills and precision, not sitting around saying "I'm the best player in the league so why do I have to work!" If the best player in the world constantly works on his game, what makes a sixteen-year-old think the world owes him anything because somebody told him he can play? Putting the time in, getting better, working on weaknesses and strengthening strengths—that's what's missing! All kids do now is play games; school ball, travel ball, club ball, more travel ball and more games! You don't get better playing games because in games you are going to do what you know how to do; good, bad, or indifferent. There is no off-season where a kid can devote six to eight weeks to work on their game and then carry that work over into the next season.

In summary, many coaches aren't coaching and developing players, some parents aren't parenting and teaching, and the kids are the ones coming up short! I was yelled at as a player. I was disciplined as a child. I believe I am a very good player and person. Stop babying your kids! Stop trying to eliminate all the pain and rejection they may face. Let them get some callouses, bruises and scrapes! It will make them tougher. Put coaches who can teach the game in positions where they can be influential to produce not only good ball players, but great people! I've been asked why I don't coach a team. It's because I have no desire to coach a team. I am here to elevate the game. My whY is to develop people *through* the game, not *for* the game!

Greatness

"Raise your right hand if you want to be good." That's a statement I often say to groups I speak to. Almost everyone raises their hand. The few who don't raise their hand usually have a sly grin on their face that implies they've heard the question before. Then I say, "Raise your left hand if you want to be GREAT." The few remaining hands go up and the ones with their hands already up laughingly plead for a re-do and I've even had a few raise both hands just to get in on "the greatness."

What does greatness look like, what does it represent, and why is it important for each of us to have our own understanding of what greatness means?

One of my favorite things to listen to is the Impact Theory Podcast hosted by Tom Bilyeu. On the show, Tom has guests from all walks of life, some famous, some not so well known. The one thing they all have in common is their greatness! Not greatness because society has labeled them as great, but because they all have their own personal vision of what greatness means to them and they live it out every day. At the end of each episode, the last question Tom asks is, "What impact do you want to have on the world?" I love that question because everyone he's interviewing displays their sincerity, belief and uniqueness in every answer.

In 2016, we witnessed greatness in the basketball world on two totally different fronts, and ironically on the same day. First, we saw Kobe Bryant, the modern-day epitome of hard work, determination and success. On the last night of the season, Kobe finished his twenty-year NBA career with sixty points, leading his woeful Laker team to a victory. Whether you love Kobe or hate him, if you understand what he has given to the game, you have no choice but to respect him. For twenty years we've watched him take shots, make shots, miss shots and take plenty of criticism along the way. However, through it all, he persevered to the top of basketball greatness again and again! I know there are many people who dislike Kobe for whatever reason. I am not one of them. I am a fan of greatness and a fan of what continued greatness requires. Salute Kobe!

Secondly, there were the Golden State Warriors. They too made history in 2016, recording seventy-three wins in one NBA season, breaking the record of seventy-two wins, set by the '95-'96 Chicago Bulls. I am a Cleveland Cavaliers fan 24/365, but much like Kobe, if you appreciate the game, you appreciate greatness! Watching the Warriors play is fun!! They play together, they move the ball, they have fun together. It doesn't matter if they already had a great team and added Kevin Durant to make the team even greater; greatness is greatness. Respect the accomplishment.

In today's culture and with the advent of social media outlets, the world is much smaller and much more connected. With the press of a button someone can send their opinion out to the masses and I believe with that we have detached ourselves from reality. When Kobe started his career twenty years ago, the core of the Warriors team was still in elementary school! There was no Twitter, Facebook, Instagram or Snapchat. Pre social media, one had to be part of press media to have their opinions heard on a broad scale. The place we're in now is a good place but we must consciously make sure we maintain our sense of true reality in a world of "unreality TV!" The reality of what true greatness is will never change; just because more people have a platform to express their opinions doesn't take away from greatness!

Determine your definition of greatness. My definition of greatness is being authentic to who you are, loving what you do, and leaving a legacy that will impact the world long after you're gone. Kobe will go down in history. So will the '15-'16 Warriors. That is greatness in my book!

Greatness will be around forever, but the funny thing is, we all understand what greatness is, but today so many people are caught up in other people's greatness, they don't recognize their own. Our current society is "connected" so much that people now latch on to someone else's greatness and claim it as their own. I'm here to remind you that other people's greatness is NOT your greatness! Of course, that doesn't mean you're not great, it simply means that the other person's greatness, no matter how famous they are, isn't for you! Determine what greatness looks like for YOU and then push towards it! LeBron's greatness is not MY greatness. If I do myself the disservice of using LeBron to compare whether I'm great, I'll always come up short. I am great because of who I am, not LeBron or anyone else!

Our attachment and desire for greatness has created a culture where people are now lowering the standards of greatness so more people can feel good about "having a piece of it." No! That's not the way it works! As I said before, greatness is greatness and will be around forever even though society has lowered the bar on how we define greatness. My suggestion to you is to study people you consider great, whoever you believe they are. Find the characteristics they possess that make them great to you. Then, in the words of my guy Tom Bilyeu, ask yourself, "What impact do YOU want to have on the world?"

Soft As Wet Toilet Tissue

I want to speak about our society and how soft we've become! We have created and enabled a culture where competition has been reserved for game situations only. What ever happened to the philosophy of competing with my teammate in a practice setting, which makes us BOTH better? It doesn't matter who plays more, we have been tested in practice and are more prepared for games because of it! There are guys who will not attend a certain school because there is a player at his position already…did you really think you were going to be the only one? Or, there are players who will leave a situation because the coaches are recruiting a player who plays his position. People—that's being soft!

I spend the majority of my days around young people. One consistency is the fact that good ol' friendly competition is almost obsolete. Athletes don't compete if they're playing twenty-one, they don't compete if they're shooting around; they don't compete… period. Everyone is "friends" now. Instagram "friends," Snapchat "friends," so the mentality has basically become *that's my friend standing in front of me, so I can take it easy on him.* Try telling that to Michael Jordan when he dunked on his "friend" Patrick Ewing in the playoffs. Or Magic Johnson who elbowed his "friend" Isaiah Thomas in the face during a game. We can be "friends" later, but right now, you are not on my team, and therefore you pose a threat!

Can competition be taught? Yes, but it must start from an internal place within the athlete and if a competitive spirit needs to be developed, I believe a GREAT coach can promote an atmosphere where healthy competition is created and encouraged. One way I personally create competition is to have "consequences" for almost everything we do during our workouts. The consequences happen whether it's a group or an individual workout. Consequences ARE NOT punishment, they are simply the result of not winning. The will to win will automatically make someone compete! I also don't refer to not winning as losing, I refer to it as "learning." So, we have Winners and Learners, because coming up short is not a loss if you learn from it!

We must teach our young people that competition is a part of life whether you're in the sports world or not. It does not go away so learning how to embrace it and become challenged by it from a healthy place, is a must!

Question: Who do young people typically learn behaviors from? Usually adults, right? So, if you're an adult reading this, my sentiment is probably speaking directly to you. If you're a youth or teen reading this book, then the sentiment is still relevant because YOU are a part of society and a culture that must work to fix the complacent, non-competitive nature we've become accustomed to.

Specifically, in the basketball space, we have created a culture where young players play way too many games! I spoke to a coach a couple of weekends ago and he told me his team played seven games in two days and the team they beat in the "championship" had just played three straight games to get there! Not only is this absurd when talking about the wear and tear on our young athletes' bodies, but it plays directly into how they mentally approach games. Any given weekend a team will have a game at nine o'clock a.m., another at one o'clock p.m., and another at six o'clock p.m. I know, they're teenagers and after all *we played all day when we were teenagers, right*? No way! We played—for real played! Today's kids are in controlled environments, complete with yelling coaches, yelling parents, and way too much unnecessary stress! We are unconsciously teaching kids to devalue the joy of winning and downplay the agony of defeat. There's always another game, another opportunity to play, so winning becomes mundane and losing doesn't hurt. As I said in a previous chapter, let's focus on development instead of how many games can be played because what inevitably happens is in your search for exposure you end up getting exposed...if you get my drift.

Another way adults have created the SOFT culture we live in is the "every Johnny gets a trophy" epidemic. This was undoubtedly created by a group of parents whose children simply weren't good enough to get an award or a trophy. This is what "participation awards" are for. "Thanks for being a part of the team, and here is your award for playing your role." Now don't get me wrong, I'm not necessarily talking about very young ages like four to ten years old, I'm talking more middle school and high school levels. When you get to those levels, there are usually clear cut "best players" and they should be recognized as such. But we've created a culture that says Johnny's feelings are hurt because he didn't get a trophy and David did. Chances are, Johnny's feelings aren't hurt, Johnny's parents' feelings are hurt! How about supporting, encouraging and being honest with yourself and your child by saying, "Here's where we came up a little short and let's figure out what we need to do to improve." But instead, we give everyone a trophy and make up awards that don't even exist to make everyone happy. And we wonder why the millennial generation feels so entitled! Well, it's because we've given them undeserved awards their whole life, so they never learn that receiving awards requires work and competition. The first time little Johnny doesn't get recognition, he is totally dumbfounded and doesn't know how to handle what he and his parents label as rejection.

Competition is part of life and I believe it should never go away. We should be on a constant pursuit of bettering ourselves; every year, every month, every day. We must teach kids how to tap into their inner competitor at an early age. We must also properly teach the beauty of external competition, which will lead to a culture of people who have intentions of getting better, value successes, and can handle setbacks. Winning isn't everything, but having a winning mentality is! Winning also isn't having the best score every time. Winning is having a clear definition of success and isn't predicated on the score. My definition of success is knowing I've done my absolute best at everything I do. And that, my friend, is a personal challenge and competition with myself! Will you embrace your personal challenge of success and competition while at the same time teaching someone else what that means?

The Menace IS Society

In life, we must learn how to master being in the valley. So often we run from the valley, but sometimes you must sit in the valley in order to learn how to climb.

Many adults talk negatively about today's generation of kids. I often hear how kids are lazy, unappreciative and have a ridiculous sense of entitlement. Please understand, I can see where millennials can get a bad rap. However, I want to explore WHY they are that way and provide an assessment of the problem from my vantage point.

As I increase my network and continue to meet people, especially young people, one thing always comes to mind: "Dang, why don't they see how good they *could* be?" People with a strong work ethic are an endangered species! We seem to have a generation of young people who think life should be handed to them. Well it will, in the form of an overhand right from Mayweather! Parents, let's look in the mirror before we blame our kids. Have you demonstrated tough love on your children? Do you hold them accountable for their actions, or do you bail them out or hand them money every time they're in a jam? My generation and those before me were brought up with tough love, but today's young people need love first! Millennials and Generation Z must be first led with love, then once they understand that the foundation for everything is love, THEN you can be as tough as you want to be. Your loving leadership of your home is not some "always nice, always happy" wonderland where there is no discipline and structure. Loving leadership is unconditional love based on respect, guidance and servant leadership. Spencer Conley, in his book *Lead with L.O.V.E.*, says it like this: "All things fall on leadership! When it's all said and done, we will see success comes down to leadership. Many of us wouldn't have made it this far without the right leadership." The success Spencer is talking about can mean your business and/or your family!

In college, I played for a guy I like to call a "Bobby Knight disciple." His name was Royce Waltman. One thing for certain, two things for sure, there were many days we walked in the gym and were called everything except a son of God! But I tell you what; we respected that man like no one else. His delivery was such that it worked for some and didn't work for others. When all was said and done, we played our hearts out for him because we knew he loved us unconditionally.

Fast forward twenty years. If he were to coach this generation of players, he wouldn't last a whole season. Years ago, a player might have quit after some time, but today the average parent is making the player quit first without a drop of sweat hitting the floor! Young people crave discipline and structure. They fight it naturally, but ultimately it is necessary for survival! STOP BABYING YOUR KIDS! Where did this gap happen? We weren't raised like this! I know full well you think, "I had to bust my hump to get here so my kid wouldn't have to work as hard." I'm here to tell you, you're not helping them, you're crippling them! Let the coach be the coach and you be there to comfort and support your child. If you want to be the coach, you should apply for the job! To all my "Original Kings of Comedy" fans, remember Bernie Mac's philosophy on parenting!

To my young people…Where is your DRIVE? Where is your PASSION? Where is your MOTIVATION to get things done? Everything WILL NOT be put right in front of your face. If you want something, you GOTTA GO GET IT! Work when others aren't working, shoot when others aren't shooting, and dribble when others aren't dribbling! You can't wait until practice to work on your game. You must develop your own relationship with the ball, with the basket and with the GAME! I love this game, everything about it! It kept me from getting in trouble as a youngster, it gave me an education, it paid me some money and it allowed me to see the world. All because I can put a ball through a basket. If you're going to say, "I love this game," then love the game, become a student of the game. There was a whole lot of basketball before Steph, LeBron and KD!! I wrote this chapter for the best player on the team AND the player who may never get in (I've been both). Work your butt off in practice, be ready to play, and when you do play, BE READY TO SHINE!

IT'S ALL ABOUT THE Y!

When the Ball Stops Bouncing...

This chapter is a contribution from my good friend, Shelby Miller. Shelby brings a fresh perspective and voice to the platform of basketball.

So, it's a Sunday night and I just got home from coaching my eighth grade girls' basketball practice. My boyfriend, Adam, wasn't home and I was feeling nostalgic so I sat down to watch some old college highlights; basically, I just wanted to relive the glory days for a bit.

And wow.

I can hardly put into words all of the feelings and emotions that instantly took over my body when I thought about college in general and my playing days. They were literally all over the spectrum. So I thought I'd put some of those emotions into words to hopefully touch at least one other person or athlete.

NEVER, EVER, EVER TAKE IT FOR GRANTED, BUT ALWAYS, ALWAYS, ALWAYS TAKE ADVANTAGE!

That sounds kind of backwards, right? No!

I say this because you shouldn't take anything for granted, ever, because you never know when it's going to be gone or over. I'm sure you've heard this many times because it's simply the truth. Don't take your teammates for granted because they graduate. Don't take your coaches for granted because they might leave and go somewhere else. Don't take your peers for granted because there's a good chance you'll/they'll graduate and you'll never see them again. Don't take people for granted because tomorrow is never promised. Don't take basketball, or your sport, for granted because some day the ball is going to stop bouncing.

I can't say I took the game for granted, but in a way I can, because I always had another opportunity to play. I always had another opportunity to learn or work with someone else. Until I didn't.

Honestly, nobody prepares you for life after your sport, and that sucks. And for me, I still struggle with finding my new identity because I've always been an athlete, a basketball player. You can read all of the books, listen to all of the podcasts you want or talk to people who have been there, but I can't say any of that helped me because I wasn't prepared. I took things for granted and assumed I'd always have another opportunity waiting for me around the corner and when I didn't, it was hard.

I say that you shouldn't take the game for granted, and you shouldn't. What you *should* do is take 100% advantage of it. Take advantage of those six a.m. practices you don't want to get up for. Take advantage of the 16s or hill sprints you're dreading. Take advantage of the seniors and their wisdom. Take advantage of the freshmen because they'll force you to think about things you haven't had to think about before. Take advantage of your coaches, mentors, athletic directors, and other coaches because there's a reason they have the title that they do. Take advantage of the long bus trips on the way home after a not so good loss. Or the bus trips that take forever because it's snowing and icing all around you. And gosh damnit take advantage of the time you have with your teammates, your roommates, and your partners in drills because that will 100% never be the same.

There's not a day that goes by that I don't wish and want to be back in college with my teammates. Of course, playing college basketball was a dream come true and I still remember just about every win and loss that ever took place, but what I remember more is my team. I remember those wins and losses because of my teammates, because of how we came back from the loss or how we celebrated the win. Thankfully, some of us are still remarkably close, but it's still not the same.

We can go out on weekends, celebrate each other's birthdays or life milestones, grab brunch to catch up or get together to watch some basketball. But it never compares to college and the way we lived our lives in those days. Our personalities haven't changed and we can still get pretty rowdy, but our way of living has changed. Life is not carefree anymore and we definitely have bigger things to worry about than passing a test, how gruesome the next practice is going to be, or how we are going to prepare for the next opponent. I truly, sincerely, wholeheartedly, and passionately miss those days more than some people could ever possibly imagine.

So…don't take the game and all that comes with it for granted and wish it was over. Because it *will* be over, faster than you can finish this sentence. Absolutely take advantage of every single minute you get. On campus, with your teammates, with your coaches, roommates, mentors, professors, long bus trips, and other athletes and friends. Because those are the moments and memories you will cling to for the rest of your life.

All About the WhY

Jayson, a somewhat unique spelling to a common name. It's funny, because for years I never really put much thought into the spelling, I just knew I despised when people spelled it wrong. Well after forty-two years on this earth, I finally figured out, It's all about the Y. In a recent conversation with my mom, she came to tears when I told her thank you for whatever inspired her to put the Y in my name, because she unknowingly solidified my PURPOSE.

"Do you." It's a phrase commonly used in modern society. It generally means "do what you do" or "stay in your lane." Well, a very personal experience allowed me to take the phrase, spin it, and make it my personal PURPOSE. My version of D.E.W. YOU as you saw in a previous section of this book originated from my dedication and memory of my father, (D)onald (E)dward (W)ells. After his passing in 2003, I had bracelets made with the statement "D.E.W. YOU" on them. The intent was simply to be a visual reminder of my childhood hero when I was on the basketball court, playing the game I loved. Though the D.E.W. YOU bracelets were made for my own personal reasons, many people started showing interest. Due to the buzz, I decided to make the acronym applicable to everyone. That's how (D)evelop (E)xtraordinary (W)inners was born.

Basketball was my outlet to stay out of trouble in the inner-city streets of Cleveland, Ohio. Drugs, gangs and other negative activity surrounded me, but my love for the game and excellent family support helped me overcome the negativity. God-given talent and an undeniable work ethic landed me a full athletic scholarship to Indiana State University. After a successful collegiate career, I was again presented with an opportunity to continue playing as a professional player internationally. Thirteen seasons, twelve different countries, and six continents later, I stand confident, passionate and ready to share my experience!

I have coined my experience "The Jayson Wells Experience." During these experiences, I touch on multiple topics and define often-misused words such as success vs significance, simple vs easy, and passion vs purpose. I believe by helping people break down these words, they can separate them and unleash the power of each. I want my audience to understand that I am just as inspired by having the opportunity to speak with them as they are inspired listening to me. I engage with others by exposing vulnerabilities from my personal experiences.

Rather than being referred to as a Motivational Speaker, I prefer to be recognized as an Experience Teller and an Empowerment Leader. I distinguish myself from other speakers with a simple yet powerful formula: as an Empowerment Leader, I add value by helping individuals, teams and leaders fill the gap between *knowing* and *doing.*

Basketball has given me the opportunity to live in Sweden, Finland, Germany, Israel, Cyprus, Korea, Holland, Italy, Ukraine, Dubai, Argentina and Australia. I have also traveled to numerous other countries like Russia, Turkey, Croatia, Austria, France, Belgium and South Africa. My travels have provided me a true appreciation of the world and have allowed me to learn about myself by learning about other cultures and people.

I've also created a curriculum-based course called "The whY Project." The Project is an eight-session course, both online and live, that will focus on an acronym I created for the word P.U.R.P.O.S.E.

➢ **Passion**

➢ **Uncommon**

➢ **Resilience**

➢ **Preparation**

➢ **Opportunity**

➢ **Service**

➢ **Experience**

More than telling people that they need to find their purpose, my desire is to help show people HOW to find their purpose. I refrain from using fear tactics, guilt trips, and talking *at* my audience. Instead, I interact and dialogue with my audience and help them identify with themselves through thought and emotion, and then use those thoughts and feelings to discover their purpose. Once people identify their *why*, value is inevitably added to their lives.

The whY Project has been designed to serve and empower people of all ages, backgrounds, and ethnicities. The program reaches out and connects with anyone who is in search of growing and learning. I am determined to empower others by educating them on what makes them individually extraordinary.

In my life, I have been blessed to see many things. In appreciation for those things, I have eliminated using the words "bad" or "good" when speaking about experience. I have learned that bad and good are just perceptions relative to the individual and usually based on external factors. There are no bad or good experiences, they are all just a part of our own unique paths which tell our own unique story.

In the same conversation with my mother when I thanked her for adding the *Y* in my name, I also asked her what her life was like raising a "basketball child." She responded, "We were never raising a basketball player, we were raising a quality person!" Now I was the one almost in tears. Because I finally gained clarity on who I am as a man and what my wh*Y* is. At the end of the day, I, too, am not raising or coaching the next generation of basketball players, I am Developing Extraordinary Winners, so they can go out and inspire and empower the world!

So please, spell my name correctly, because it's all about the wh*Y*…

Misunderstood

Michael Jordan, Magic Johnson, Larry Bird, Isaiah Thomas and Patrick Ewing. What do these guys all have in common besides being Hall of Fame players? They were all great friends off the court but would do whatever was needed to within the rules (and some outside) to beat any of the others. Kevin Garnett has always been my favorite player of my generation for that same reason. All in all, every guy on this list has so much passion for what they do, it seems to literally pour out on the floor. But…

Where has the heart gone? Where has the passion gone? Can you teach the qualities that the legends possessed to today's players? Can you teach young players passion? I don't know about you, but even now, my competitive nature is so strong that I must suppress it to the point of letting my sons win at wrestling sometimes. My observation—today's athletes don't demonstrate the emotion for the game they say they love. I believe if you love something, there is always a passion to fight, a passion to want more and a passion to show pride in what you do. One word of encouragement I received that will always stick with me is, "In sport you will not always be number one but for goodness sake, at the end of the day, the other team WILL know they were in a fight!" I have never seen a bunch of athletes "lay down" so quickly in my life like I see in today's athletes.

Throughout the course of my career, I have been called crazy, labeled a troublemaker, and ultimately missed out on playing opportunities because my passion was misunderstood. Competition runs through my veins 24/7 and I DESPISE losing. During my playing years, if I felt like a teammate, coach or anyone else was preventing us from being able to win…they knew it because I LET them know it! Thankfully, I have learned through experience that there is a certain way to communicate. But as a young passionate player striving to prove himself, sometimes my delivery method got lost. I'm going to drop some complete openness and vulnerability on you.

On my right forearm, I have a scar. I look down at it every day and feel embarrassed, ashamed and blessed all at the same time. It happened the only time I totally lost my composure concerning anything in my life. I was in Finland, it was my second year as a pro, and we had just lost our fifth road game in a row. While waiting to shake hands with the other team, my team decided to have a "let's stick together meeting" behind me. My coach yelled out to the court, "See, that's why we can't win, because you are too concerned with the other team!" That, my friends, may be the worst thing you can ever say to me as a competitor; because no matter the situation (and I've been in some bad ones) my team is ALWAYS my number one priority. Well, after an exchange of unpleasant words, we walked back to the locker room area and I literally lost my marbles and punched what I thought was a wall. Turned out it was not a wall, it was a glass door. Fifty-four stitches later, tears rolling down my face, thankful I hadn't ruined my whole career, I vowed to never put myself anywhere close to that position again.

My arm healed. I only missed one game due to that injury; however, the learning experience was priceless. I knew I had to find a way to channel my emotions into positive energy and NEVER let anyone push me that far again! After all, passion to the extent I showed it can only be perceived as negative. What *didn't* change after that night was my passion and intensity for the game I love. Since then I have had teammates say I was too hard on them, coaches who thought I was a rebel, and other teams that would not sign me because they thought I was a troublemaker. All because I love to win! That's how I work, and I *thought* that was the definition of a TEAM. A group of people, with a common cause, who have the responsibility to be accountable for their part and to hold others accountable as well. I tell you what—it gets old very quick being the "cheerleader" AND the "go to" guy on the team. So, when I stopped being the energy source, letting my passion overflow, I was then criticized for not having the fire anymore! What's a guy to do? Each person on the team should be responsible for getting themselves ready for battle, and, as you know, every person requires something different to get ready. I know for myself, sometimes being in a playful, laughing mood was what I needed. Other times I looked like I wanted to take on the world with 2Pac. Bottom line, get it done however you need to.

Passion is another area that reflects the general state we are in as a culture today. I believe there are two huge reasons for lack of passion. (1) Our young people constantly see and hear a society of people who are not passionate about what they do because they don't love what they are doing! (2) We have babied our young people so much that when they do run across someone truly passionate, many times that passion is viewed as crazy because that person is exercising so much emotion.

I am still very passionate about the game of basketball. I am also very passionate about sharing my experiences and things I have learned so I can help other people, especially our young people. I was raised being told that in order to be happy in the workplace you must be passionate and love what you do, work your passion in some extraordinary place, and make sure your passion helps someone else! How awesome is that? I heard Maya Angelou once say, "If you learn something, teach something! At our best, we are all teachers."

One of my favorites is a quote originally attributed to Confucius: "If you love what you do for a living, you will never WORK a day in your life!" My advice to everyone would be to study the difference between passion and purpose. Often, they are used synonymously, but they are not synonyms. Have you taken time to reflect and discover what your passion is AND what your purpose is?

I have discovered my PURPOSE, the reason WHY I put my feet down every morning. It's an awesome feeling to KNOW the reason you are on this Earth.

Reward and Expectation

We all love our kids, and we want to see them happy and fulfilled. But we are robbing them of the experiences that make life memorable and make them capable, responsible and confident adults. For those of us who had a few nice things as teenagers, we probably purchased those things with money we earned after saving for some ungodly amount of time. Now, we give our children almost everything and the crazy part is it's not explicitly for them, it's to make us look good and validate what great parents we are! The bottom line is that we tend to not value something we were given, as much as something we worked for.

There were lessons in our experiences, even though we didn't know it at the time. All those situations we had to figure out, and battles with teachers we clashed with, played out as opportunities for us to learn how to compromise and handle conflict resolution. It also taught us that the world isn't fair. Sometimes people just don't like you and sometimes you'll work your butt off and still get screwed. However, most of us left high school as problem solvers. Nowadays, our kids are leaving high school with Mommy and Daddy on speed dial.

Kids don't have the "balls" of their parents. We aren't prepared to tell our kids that if they don't work for something, they won't have it. All because we can't stand to see them go without and we can't stand to see them fail. We give them a whole lot of stuff…stuff that will break down, wear out, get lost, go out of style and lose value.

As parents, I suppose some of you feel proud about how you've contributed in a material way to your kid's popularity and paved an easy street for them. I also know there are many of you who are just as frustrated as I am. I worry about what we've robbed our kids of in the process of giving them everything.

Here are five critical life skills every kid needs to learn:

1. **Delayed gratification is a GOOD thing.** It teaches you perseverance and how to determine the true value of something. Our kids don't know a damn thing about delayed gratification. To them, delayed gratification is waiting for their phone to charge.

2. **Problem solving skills and the ability to manage emotion are crucial life skills.** Kids nowadays have every problem solved for them. Good luck calling their college professor to argue about how your child, I mean young adult, should have another shot at that final because they had two other finals to study for and were stressed. Don't laugh, it's been done!!

3. **Independence allows you to discover who you really are instead of being what someone else expects you to be.** Independence was something I craved. I would have survived off Ramen noodles and gallon juices to maintain my independence. Oh wait, I actually did that. Today's kids have traded independence for new cars and iPhones. They are perfectly fine living under someone's thumb forever, if it means cool stuff. It's absurd! You're supposed to WANT to grow up and go explore the world; not live on someone else's dime, under someone else's rule and very often these days, under someone else's roof.

4. **Common sense is that little something extra that allows you to figure out how to change a tire, or not to be in a certain neighborhood after a certain time!** You develop common sense by making mistakes and learning from them. It's a skill best acquired in a setting where it's safe to fail and is only mastered

by doing things for yourself. By micromanaging our kids all the time, we're setting them up for a lifetime of cluelessness. At a certain age, that cluelessness becomes dangerous!

5. **Mental toughness is what allows a person to keep going despite everything going wrong.** People with mental toughness are the ones who come out on top. They battle through job losses, difficult relationships, illness and failure. It is a quality born from adversity. Adversity is a GOOD thing. It teaches you what you're made of. It puts into practice the old saying "What doesn't kill you makes you stronger." It's life's teacher.

I know you're probably calling me names right now or thinking of all the reasons this doesn't apply to you and your kid, but I couldn't care less what you think of me. My goal is to encourage you to at least think about doing things a different way. Personal accountability and responsibility are the most loving things you can teach your kids. I have kids and yes, they have access to things I didn't have at their age, but they also understood at a very early age the difference between reward and expectation! I'm also certainly not saying that our parents did everything right—God knows all that secondhand smoke I was exposed to, along with the unwarranted beatdowns, were less than ideal.

I do think parents in the seventies and eighties defined their roles in a way we never have. I worry that our kids are leaving home with more intellectual ability than we did, but without the life skills that will give them the success and independence that we enjoyed!

You've Got 24 Hours to Live

"If you had twenty-four hours to live, how would you spend your time and with whom? Let's be open and honest."

For the last year or so, I've asked myself the same question every morning as my feet touch the floor: If today was my last day on Earth, is what I'm about to do how I really want to go out? Talk about an honest moment. Think for a moment about what that question does for you personally. It should automatically give you a sense of purpose and focus. Think about how many things we do daily that have absolutely no contribution to anything or anyone. Or better yet, think about how many things we do during the day that are based on something that happened yesterday or we think will happen tomorrow.

Books like *The Power of Now* and *Live in the Moment* and the myriad quotes we come across say the same exact thing. YESTERDAY IS GONE and TOMORROW ISN'T PROMISED. We all know this, but we don't live like it. We live like we've always got time to make things right, or we'll do that thing when the time is right. The only time ANYTHING is right is NOW! Now is the only time we can affect yet we attempt to spend all our time in other places.

Whatever you happen to call your Supreme Being is up to you, but I personally believe in God. I've found myself in conversations with others about how God doesn't speak to us like He spoke to people in Bible days. I completely disagree! I believe God speaks to us constantly. I also believe that we can only hear God when we are calm and still, yet when are we calm and still? When we are PRESENT, in the NOW!

Technology is making our lives even worse. Most of us spend most of our day with our phone in our hand. Talk about being robbed of being in the moment. We scroll, tap, like and follow people and things that we don't even know instead of enjoying the things and people that are directly in front of us. Every time we pick up our phone in the presence of other people, it's basically saying, "I don't want to be here with you, I'd rather be somewhere else!" I was in a restaurant the other day and there were about twenty people in line ahead of me and sixteen of them where scrolling on their phone. That's eighty percent! I really like this one: while at a friend's birthday party recently, I saw a young lady swiping on a dating site. I understand online dating is commonplace, but I couldn't help think that maybe if she put her phone down and actually interacted with the people she was in the same room with, maybe she could find who she was looking for.

If you lived every day like it was your last you would automatically engage in activities that were intentional and that served a purpose; activities that would hopefully leave a legacy to let someone know you were here. You would eliminate all the things that didn't matter. And why? BECAUSE THEY DON'T MATTER! Waking up with a PURPOSE has literally changed my life. I have different levels of purpose; some involve my family and friends, some involve goals I will accomplish within the athletic industry, and some are simply enhancements I desire to see in the world. Either way, I've found that purposeful living has given me a daily road map to the places I want to go and reinforced beliefs that I have.

At the end of each day I ask myself another question. I say, "I just traded twenty-four hours of my life away. Am I happy with what I got in return?" If I find that the answer is "no" a few days in a row, it's a bold reminder that I need to live in the now, with intention!

The day you are living in right now will never come again—live like you really know what that means. Focus on what is important to you. Is it family and friends, or is it an idea that's been burning inside you, or is it executing the path that will leave your legacy for years to come? Whatever your answer, start living today like it's the last day you'll ever be able to do that one thing, or love that person, or accomplish that goal!

About the Author

Jayson Wells is a winner. He has traveled the world and inspired youth globally with his personal mission to Develop. Extraordinary. Winners. Growing up in Cleveland, Ohio, Jayson never dreamed he would play professionally in twelve different countries after playing basketball at Indiana State University and earning a degree in Sport Management.

Jayson struggled early as a player, often having to sit on the bench behind more experienced players. These early struggles tested Jayson's commitment to his goals and ignited a passion within him to maximize his potential. His growth spurt combined with a tenacity to develop as a player opened up a world of opportunities and launched a successful career.

In 2011, Jayson retired from playing basketball and shifted his focus to teaching the game he loves. He teamed up with Nike to facilitate various skills academies throughout the country, and has also worked with Kevin Durant, LeBron James and Kyrie Irving at their elite basketball camps. Determined to reach more youth globally, Jayson founded the Shooting Starz Academy, a youth development organization that provides character building in addition to athletic training. Jayson uses his personal experience to teach the core values of life to youth, on and off the court. He attributes his positive mindset to the lessons he learned from his father who taught him a strong work ethic, positive attitude, and focused discipline.

Jayson regularly delivers presentations and workshops to individuals, teams and organizations, guiding them on how to win "Beyond The Game." His presentations challenge listeners to discover their "purpose" and ignite their legacy through "significance."

Jayson Wells

Acknowledgements

I'd like to thank my wonderful mom Pauline AKA Mama Wells. Thank you for instilling in me the values and principles that have guided me through my life, both athletically and non-athletically. Thank you to my dad, Donald, who showed me what true manhood looked like, not according to societal norms. To all my aunts, uncles, cousins and friends, I thank you for the role each of you played in my development from a boy into a man. Thank you!

To Sherman Dillard, Doc Conroy, Chris Theobald, Greg Lansing and Eric "ED" Dennis, words will never be able to do justice to how instrumental each of you are in my life. You took a chance on a skinny kid from Cleveland who had no other Division I offers. You were patient as I developed and improved, you taught, led and poured into me on and off the court. You gave me a way out... For that I am eternally grateful.

To Royce Waltman, Dick Bender, and Rick Ray. Yes, it was only one season, but what a season it was. You took me from a kid who played basketball to a young man who knew HOW TO PLAY BASKETBALL. And to think, it almost didn't happen... Thank you!!

To every coach and teammate I had as a professional, thank you! Thank you for dealing with a young man who didn't know how to channel his emotions for most of his career. Thank you for the opportunity to expand my horizons, see the world, and meet people who would forever impact my life... Thank you!

To Angel, thank you for being who you are. A great person, a great woman and a wonderful mother to our two boys. I thank you for being a part of my life.

Magic, words don't even begin to express what you've added to my life. You are dreams come true, fantasies to reality, prayers answered. You have taken me to a level of life and love that most think are just fairy tales. You push me, support me, lead me to accountability. You pray with me and for me. You allow me to be your rock just as much as you are mine. I love you with all my heart, it's an honor to be yours...831.

To Jaylen and Jaydon, you are the reasons I decided to write this book. I have been blessed to live so much life and I want my life to be the catapult for your lives. See the world, meet people, love hard, take risks, fall...and get back up, LIVE LIFE!!! Do what YOU want to do, not what I, or ANYONE else thinks you should do. If it's basketball, I'll teach you everything I know. If it's something else, I'll love and support you the way only a dad can. Think with PURPOSE, move with PURPOSE, LIVE with PURPOSE... I love you!!!

Thank you to Michelle Hill, *Your Legacy Builder* at Winning Proof, my book collaborator. Michelle and her team of professionals provided the expertise and tools to make this book possible: Michael Scott, thank you for creating a captivating cover design; Michael LaRocca, for your expert proofreading and editing; and finally my publisher, Drew Becker of Realization Press, for your expertise and knowledge that pushed me over the finish line.

How to Order

<u>To book Jayson Wells</u> for your next team, employee, or leadership meeting, conference, retreat, or convention, <u>to order bulk copies</u>, or <u>to request media interviews</u>:

Website: **www.jaysonwells.com**

Email: **jayson@jaysonwells.com**

If you're a fan of this book, please tell others...

- Write about *The Things We Know But Do Not Do* on your blog and social media channels.

- Suggest this book to your friends, family, neighbors, and coworkers.

- Write a positive review on Amazon.com.

- Purchase additional copies for your business or sports team, or to give away as gifts.

- Feature Jayson on your radio or television broadcast.

CPSIA information can be obtained
at www.ICGtesting.com
Printed in the USA
FFHW010637070919
54842814-60534FF